# In Defense of My
## *Life of Jesus*

# IN DEFENSE OF MY
# *Life of Jesus*
## AGAINST THE HEGELIANS

*by*

## David Friedrich Strauss

*Translated, edited,
and with an introduction by*
Marilyn Chapin Massey

*Archon Books*
*1983*

First published 1983 as an Archon Book,
an imprint of The Shoe String Press Inc.,
Hamden, Connecticut 06514
Printed in the United States of America

The paper in this book meets the guidelines
for performance and durability of the Committee
on Production Guidelines for Book Longevity
of the Council on Library Resources.

Library of Congress Cataloging in Publication Data

Strauss, David Friedrich, 1808–1874.
　　In defense of my Life of Jesus against the
Hegelians.
　　　　Translation of: Streitschriften zur Vertheidigung
meiner Schrift über das Leben Jesu und zur Charakteris-
tik der gegenwärtigen Theologie.
　　　　Bibliography: p.
　　　　1. Strauss, David Friedrich, 1808–1874. Das leben
Jesu. 2. Jesus Christ—Biography. I. Title.
BT301.S74A313 1983　　　232.9'01　　　83-10644
ISBN 0-208-02017-9

# CONTENTS

*Acknowledgments*   vii

Introduction   ix

In Defense of My *Life of Jesus* against the Hegelians

   I. The General Relation of the Hegelian
      Philosophy to Theological Critique   3

  II. Hegel's Opinion on the Historical
       Value of the Gospel History   21

 III. Different Christological Directions
       within the Hegelian School   38

*Selected Bibliography*   67

*Index*   71

# ACKNOWLEDGMENTS

James A. Massey worked with me on the first draft of this translation; his expertise in the language of German idealism made an invaluable contribution to this final version. I am also grateful to Professor Peter C. Hodgson, who offered general encouragement throughout the course of this project.

# INTRODUCTION

## Historical Background

Heinrich Heine (1799-1865), writing about Germany to a French audience in 1834, boldly declared, "it is important at the moment to neutralize the power of religion. You see, we Germans are in the same situation as you were before the revolution, when Christianity and the old regime formed an absolutely inseparable alliance. This could not be destroyed as long as Christianity still exerted its influence on the masses. Voltaire had to start up his cutting laughter before Samson [the executioner in Paris during the French Revolution] could let his axe fall."[1] The following year a German Voltaire did appear in the person of David Friedrich Strauss (1808-74), the author of the most celebrated book on religion of the nineteenth century, *The Life of Jesus, Critically Examined.*[2] From his desk at Tübingen University, the twenty-six-year-old seminary teacher brought together the most cherished possession of Protestant Germany, the Bible, with its most significant nineteenth-century cultural product, the philosophy of George Wilhelm Friedrich Hegel (1770-1831), into a form that exploded in Germany like a lightening bolt and cleared the way for the left-wing Hegelian movement that culminated in the work of Karl Marx (1818-83).[3]

*The Life of Jesus* evoked "panic-striken terror" in the breasts of the defenders of the political *status quo* and images of the proximity of Satan in souls of the defenders of Christian orthodoxy.[4] To these two groups, the book was a symbol of sedition and heresy, and they directed at it an extraordinary barrage of criticism. In contrast, to a third group, composed of young and discontented intellectuals and students of Hegel, such as Arnold Ruge (1802-82), Ludwig Feuerbach (1804-72), and Marx, *The Life of Jesus* was a symbol of the right to criticize freely the religious and political orders. Strauss's defense of *The Life of Jesus* against the more moderate Hegelians who rejected it became the philosophical charter document of left-wing Hegelianism. *In Defense of My "Life of Jesus"*,[5] published in 1837, spells out, in a way that *The Life of Jesus* did not, the elements of a *Hegelian critique*, of the necessity and the right of examining the claims of *any* phenomena to be true. The work of a Christian theologian, *In Defense* declared that even theology must be critique and not a mere translation of the doctrines of Christianity into relevant cultural terms.

## The Impact of *The Life of Jesus*

*The Life of Jesus* itself is that rare instance of a serious scholarly investigation that also captures the popular imagination. In over eight hundred pages of systematic analysis, liberally sprinkled with Greek and Hebrew phrases, *The Life of Jesus* tested the Gospels of the New Testament for their historical validity. It concluded that most of the narratives cannot be verified as truly historical and that they are myth, that is, unconscious poetic creations of the earliest Christians, who shaped stories about Jesus to express their belief in him as the Messiah promised to Israel. The scholarly weight of *The Life of Jesus* was such that it shaped the modern academic discipline of biblical criticism, where even today it functions as a limit to be emulated or rejected. Along with Marx and the left-wing Hegelians, eminent figures like George Eliot, who translated it into English, and countless ministers, who translated its erudition into a simple message for their congregations, helped *The Life of Jesus* burst out of the walls of academe and gain the influence to affect the course of world history.[6]

The immediately obvious reason for its apocalyptic effect is that it raised a crucial question for Christian faith: What does the demonstration of the mythical nature of most of the gospel narratives about Jesus mean for the truth of faith in Christ as God's son? In the final few pages of *The Life of Jesus* Strauss provided his own answer, an answer that significantly enhanced its potency to startle its times. The recognition of the mythical nature of the gospel story of Jesus means nothing for Christian faith except its development to a fuller, freer stage. To see that the Jesus of actual first-century history is not identical with the Christ of Christian faith leads to the discovery of the true identity of Christ. Christians have always struggled to understand the Christ of faith, how he is truly God and truly man, one person with two natures. *The Life of Jesus* ends the struggle. By dissociating Christ from the single human Jesus, it frees Christians to see that the true identity of Christ is the Hegelian idea of the human species.

To the simple Christian believer unschooled in academic theology or philosophy, *The Life of Jesus* came as a shock so intense that some did indeed associate it with the apocalypse. Yet to the educated, to the theologian and philosopher of the early nineteenth century, the book said nothing essentially new. Biblical scholars had been questioning the historical validity of the gospel stories since at least the time of Hermann Samuel Reimarus (1696-1768), the author of the famous *Wolfenbüttel Fragments* published by Gotthold Lessing (1728-81). Innumerable European philosophers, including Germany's own Lessing and Immanuel Kant (1724-1804), had been offering ideas and ideals of humanity in the place of the believer's Christ for over a century. Why then did the book so inspire some and "strike panic-stricken terror" in others? While there are many aspects to an adequate explanation to this question, the central one is the one before us in Strauss's 1837 *Defense*—the claim that *The Life of Jesus* was a product of and consistent with the principles of Hegelianism.

Before the publication of *The Life of Jesus*, Hegelianism was the official philosophy of the government of Prussia, the leading Protestant state among the thirty-nine that made up Germany. Hegelianism provided the rationale for those attempting to restore the order and privileges of monarchy in Germany in the wake of the changes brought by Napoleon; this rationale supported hereditary monarchy and linked this form of government with true religion. Essential to the Hegelian philosophy's political role, then, was its claim to reconcile traditional, orthodox Christianity with modern thought. Indeed, this is a claim that some contemporary Christian theologians still find viable, even though the Hegelian philosophy in now removed by a century and a half from the sociopolitical conditions of its genesis and political utility. In 1835, however, just at the time when Germany was feeling the aftershocks of the Paris Revolution of 1830 and when such less-than-loyal subjects as Heine were calling for a German revolution, the viability of its claim to reconcile orthodox Christianity and modern thought was inexorably united with its political utility. The appearance of *The Life of Jesus* undermined this claim and initiated the criticism of religion in Germany that Marx was to call "the presupposition of all criticism."[7]

## The Hegelian Theologians

Strauss's defense of *The Life of Jesus* against its Hegelian critics thus holds the key to the enormous impact of the book. At the outset of *In Defense* he states that he was not at all surprised that, upon the publication of *The Life of Jesus*, "the many opponents of the Hegelian philosophy used its conclusions to demonstrate the destructive consequences of the Hegelian philosophy" or that the Hegelian school moved "to reject the point of view of my book and protect itself from being identified with it" (p.7). The threat to the reputation of Hegelianism was indeed so severe that the Prussian minister of education, Baron Karl von Altenstein (1770-1840), asked the theologian Carl Friedrich Göschel (1784-1862) to salvage it by refuting *The Life of Jesus*.[8] Göschel is named in the *Defense* as belonging to the wing of the Hegelian school that Strauss called the right, using the analogy of the political positions within the French Parliament. George Andreas Gabler (1786-1853) and the quixotic Bruno Bauer (1809-82), who later became for a brief time a colleague of Marx, are also named on the right.

The characteristic of this right wing was its attempt to derive the historical validity of *all* of the biblical narratives from the philosophical comprehension of the truth of Christianity. It should be noted that, although Strauss used a political analogy in naming the division of the Hegelian school, he did not explicitly draw out the political parallels to the positions. Many of his contemporaries, however—including of course Altenstein and those who would join Strauss on the left wing—did. The obvious parallel to the right-wing theological position is the politically right-wing goal of legitimating the hereditary monarchy by a philosophical comprehension of its truth. Even before the appearance of *The Life of Jesus*, influential Prussians questioned the capability of Hegelianism to provide this legitimation, insisting that a direct assertion of the biblical God's will was a more evident and effective basis for a secure government than was Hegelianism, which, in stressing reflective thought, left room for liberal rationalism.

Karl Rosenkranz (1805-79), the noted biographer of Hegel, is a representative of this politically liberal potential in Hegelianism. Strauss expresses admiration for his fairness and his openness to the thought of Friedrich Schleiermacher (1763-1834), the founder of "liberal" theology, which gives up elements of orthodoxy as unessential to faith. Strauss places Rosenkranz alone at the center of the Hegelian school. An attempt to verify only a part of the biblical history from the truth of the philosophical idea constitutes this center position. Strauss opposes even the theologically liberal Rosenkranz, however, because Strauss takes his stand, also alone at first, on the left wing of the school, where he holds that *no* biblical history can be accepted as valid without being tested by historical critique. The political parallel to this left-wing theological stand is found in the history of the Hegelians who preceded Marx. The publication of *In Defense* provided the death blow to Hegelianism's political respectability. In the years from 1837 to 1844, however, Hegelian critique gained force in both religion and politics.

*In Defense* puts before us the principles by which Strauss dismantled one of modernity's most significant interpretations of the meaningfulness of Christian orthodoxy, and thereby planted the roots of its most influential criticism of religion. An examination of *The Life of Jesus* and of the elements of the Hegelian philosophy, as well as of the structure and highlights of *In Defense* itself, will serve to further introduce the text.

## The Hegelian Question of *The Life of Jesus*

When one reads *The Life of Jesus*, its Hegelianism can seem to be almost a *deus ex machina*, introduced only at the very end to save the truth of Christianity. Strauss writes explicitly about this philosophy only in his final discussion of how Christians are to identify Christ truly once his identification with Jesus of Nazareth is lost. In the *Defense*, however, Strauss tells us that Hegelianism shaped the earlier work from the beginning. Most important, he relates that his entire enterprise was motivated by a question raised for him by Hegel's promise to reconcile religion and philosophy; Hegel claimed that he would accomplish this with the aid of a distinction between religious representation and philosophical concept. Hegel held that the *forms* of the representation and of the concept differed, but their *content* was the same. The content of the Christian representation, the incarnation of God in Christ, is the same as the content of the philosophical concept, indeed of absolute truth itself; thus, religion and philosophy are not enemies, as they had seemed to be for many enlightened intellectuals in the eighteenth century, but rather they are reconciled.

Strauss wanted to know what this distinction meant with regard to "the historical components of the Bible, especially the Gospels" (p. 3). Does their historical character belong to the content or to the form of the representation? Does speculative reason have to comprehend as history what is reported in the story of the life of Jesus as part of the content common to religion and philosophy? Does Hegel's reconciliation between religion and philosophy call for a repression of the doubts inevitably experienced by any nineteenth-century cultured person, aware of the advances of the natural sciences, when he or she reads about the miracles in the Gospels? Hegel had not directly answered these questions, but his theological disciples, most notably the University of Berlin theologian Philip Conrad Marheineke (1780-1864), seemed to answer yes. *The Life of Jesus* was motivated by an attempt to answer no.

We will look more closely in the next section at the elements of Hegel's philosophy that bear on the debate occasioned by the answer given in *The Life of Jesus*, but first we will let *The Life of Jesus* speak for itself. In this way, the issues it raises can unfold with the force and drama that they presented to Strauss's contemporaries.

The object of *The Life of Jesus, Critically Examined* is simple and straightforward: to investigate whether the story of the life of Jesus narrated in the Gospels is historically accurate. Nothing illustrates this more clearly than the fact that the book is organized chronologically, moving from the stories of Jesus' birth to his loss in the temple, on through his public mission to his death, and finally to the stories of his resurrection and ascension. Contemporary biblical scholars agree with Strauss's premise that there is insufficient evidence to assume that the Gospels were written by eyewitnesses, but, given this, they most often go on to investigate the history of the gospel stories, tracing them back as far as possible in the process of story telling about Jesus, perhaps even to Jesus himself.

In contrast, Strauss was not directly interested in the history of the genesis of the stories but in whether the stories as they stood were historical. Obviously, these two historical approaches are not entirely distinct. Nevertheless, in most cases, even when a contemporary biblical scholar traces a story all the way back to a locus in Jesus' life, the verifiable history he or she finds there is different from the story as it stands in the Gospels and as it has been literally interpreted in traditional Christianity. In a sense, it is the traditional interpretations of the stories that primarily concern Strauss. In the *Defense* he tells us that he had at first planned to write an entire first part of *The Life of Jesus* that would have contained an "objective presentation of the life of Jesus according to the evangelists, next a presentation of the way Jesus lives in the subjective hearts of the believers, and, finally, the mediation of these two sides in the second article of the Apostles' Creed," the confession that Jesus Christ is the Son of God (p.5). Although Strauss does not use the term "representation" himself, these three components—an objective element, subjective faith, and a reflective content such as is found in the creeds—belong to religious representation.

Strauss also tells us that he joined this first part to his historical critique. This procedure can be seen in his beginning the investigation of each incident of Jesus' life by calling to mind the traditional, orthodox interpretation of these narratives. He does not merely repeat the literal words of the Gospels themselves. He starts with what is believed at the most immediate level about the story of Jesus' life;

that is, he begins with the representation. Only as a second step does Strauss review the text of the Gospels. In a third step, he moves to review contemporary interpretations of the historical nature of the actual narratives. He shows how supernaturalists, those who defend the notion of direct divine intervention in history, explain the historical element in the narratives and how rationalist or naturalist interpreters, those who accept an action of God only through the laws of nature, explain it. Finally, he gives his own judgment. In most cases it is that the gospel narrative is myth.

## Religious Representation and the Story of the Virgin Birth

The right-wing and center Hegelian theological treatment of the virgin birth of Jesus Christ is a central topic in the *Defense*, and therefore we will use Strauss's analysis of it in *The Life of Jesus* to illustrate the basic procedure he uses throughout the book. He begins by recalling the coherent story developed in Christian tradition to explain that the gospel accounts of the conception of Jesus mean "that Jesus was conceived in Mary not by a human father, but by the Holy Ghost."[9] Made so familiar to Christians in art and song, this story begins with the announcement by an angel to the aged and barren Joachim and Anna that they will have a daughter who will be the mother of God. This child, Mary, is dedicated to God by her graced parents and lives in the temple tended by angels until she is presented for betrothal by the high priest. This priest identifies Joseph, who is himself of advanced age, as Mary's spouse. He is selected from among all the unmarried men of the House of David because his staff flowers. Joseph and Mary do not consummate their marriage, and while he is away on business the angel Gabriel appears to her and announces that she is to bear the Son of God. Mary does not tell Joseph about this, and he becomes disturbed when he learns she is pregnant. Then an angel appears to him in a dream to reveal that Mary has conceived her child by the Holy Ghost.[10]

Strauss proceeds next to compare this story with the gospel texts themselves. There are only two gospel accounts, Matthew 1:18-25 and Luke 1:5-80. Matthew narrates only the angel's revelation to Joseph in a dream, and Luke narrates only Gabriel's announcement to Mary. Strauss maintains that those biblical interpreters who try to remain faithful to the text have difficulty reconciling these two stories into a probable history. Initially he asks how a cultured, reflective person of the nineteenth century is to interpret these texts *even if* he or she suspends questions about the miraculous content of the accounts. For example, how can one make sense of the fact that the angel talking to Joseph acts as if he were the first messenger to reveal the occurrence and says nothing about a revelation to Mary? The major question, however, is this: If Mary had been told first, why did she keep silent, risking her reputation and causing pain for Joseph?

For answers to these queries about the consistency of the two accounts Strauss turns to the work of contemporary interpreters. At this point he emphasizes the interpretations of supernaturalist theologians, who, because they accept the historical possibility of miracles, do not have severe problems explaining the miraculous content of the narratives. Yet they have problems explaining discrepancies between the forms of the two narratives, the two revelations, and Mary's silence. Strauss cites one supernaturalist who speculated, "It must have cost Mary much self-denial to have concealed the communication from Joseph; and this reserve, in a matter known only to herself and to God, must be regarded as a proof of her firm trust in God. . . . [She must have thought:] Had it been intended that Joseph should have participated in the communication, the angel would have appeared to him, too." At this point, Strauss comments, "If each individual favored with a divine revelation were of this opinion, how many special revelations would it not require." According to the interpreter, Mary also thought, "Besides, it is an affair of God alone, consequently it becomes me to leave it with him to convince Joseph." Again Strauss interjects a witty side comment, calling this "the argument of indolence." Finally, Strauss cites another supernaturalist who agrees in attributing Mary's silence to her piety and who adds "that in relation to events so extraordinary the measure of the ordinary occurrences of the world is not applicable." To this Strauss remarks that it is common delicacy and propriety which do not apply![11]

Rationalist interpreters, who like the supernaturalists try to maintain that the gospel narratives are historical, have the same problems as the latter in dealing with the form of the accounts, but they also have difficulties with their miraculous content. What they attempt to do is supply a rational explanation for miraculous events which in fact happened naturally but were not properly explained by the scientifically unsophisticated evangelists. Their questions press the historical improbability of the accounts one step further, because they are faced with explaining "a most remarkable deviation from natural laws," a virgin birth. Strauss comments: "However obscure the physiology of the fact [of human conception], it is proved by an exceptionless experience that only by the concurrence of the two sexes is a new human being generated."[12] Given this incontrovertible natural fact, the rationalists are driven to explain the narratives as did the most eminent of them, H. E. G. Paulus (1761-1851), who wrote, "Prior to her union with Joseph, Mary, under the influence of a pure enthusiasm in the sacred things on the one hand, and by a human cooperation pleasing to God on the other, became the mother of a child who on account of this holy origin was to be called a son of God."[13]

We can now begin to understand the effectiveness of *The Life of Jesus*. Its readers, first asked to recall the treasured story of Joachim, Anna, Joseph with his flowering staff, Mary, and the angel Gabriel, are led on to consider a series of absurdities which culminate in the suggestion that the historical truth of the virgin birth is Mary's brief, enthusiastic extramarital affair. This dissolution of the stories of Jesus' life is repeated over and over again, and in each case the reader is left seeking a way out of the rubble of ridiculous explanations, back to some sort of meaning.

Strauss was prepared to supply this meaning in the form of the mythical explanation. In the case of the virgin birth, he explained:

> In the world of mythology many great men had extraordinary births and were sons of the gods. Jesus himself spoke of his heavenly origin and called God his father; besides his title as Messiah was Son of God. From Matthew

[1:22], it is further evident that the passage of Isaiah [7:14] was referred to Jesus by the early Christian Church. In conformity with this passage the belief prevailed that Jesus, as the Messiah, should be born of a virgin by means of divine agency; it was therefore taken for granted that what was to be actually did occur; and thus originated a philosophical (dogmatical) mythus concerning the birth of Jesus.[14]

In conclusion Strauss declares, "But according to historical truth, Jesus was the offspring of an ordinary marriage between Joseph and Mary," and he stresses that the mythical view, in contrast to the interpretations of the supernaturalists and the rationalists, "maintains at once the dignity of Jesus and the respect due to his Mother."[15] There is no doubt that, for the reader who finds himself or herself caught up in the argumentation of *The Life of Jesus*, Strauss's mythical interpretation offers a temporary sense of relief by retrieving a real and dignified human Jesus. But what has happened to the Christ of faith?

The answer to this question is given by the Hegelian philosophy in the conclusion of *The Life of Jesus*. Before we look at it, it is important to emphasize that the historical critique prepares directly, if not explicitly, for the Hegelian solution. What is achieved laboriously in the long first part of the book is a recognition that Christian religious representations are not records of objective *facts*. They do have an objective element, because they are early Christian *ideas* that are expressed in the form of historical narratives.[16] The early Christian community "stimulated by the person and fate of Jesus . . . shaped its picture of Christ having in mind unconsciously the idea of humanity in relation to Divinity."[17] From that time on, Christians have struggled to comprehend these representations. Now, freed by the knowledge that they are not history, nineteenth-century believers can move on to comprehend fully their true content by means of Hegel's philosophy.

## The Philosophical Concept and the Doctrine of Christ

Strauss begins the concluding section of *The Life of Jesus* with his own promise of reconciliation—"to re-establish dogmatically that which has been destroyed critically." Again he turns to the religious representation as the point of concern in this reconciliation.

> Hitherto our criticism had for its object the content of Christianity as historically presented in the gospel records; now this content having been called into question in its historical form assumes the form of a mental product and finds a refuge in the soul of the believer where it exists, not as a simple history but as a reflected history, that is, a confession of faith, a received dogma. Against this dogma appearing in its immediacy *criticism as a form of negativity and of the struggle for mediation* must certainly arise just as it must arise against any immediacy. Thus this criticism is no longer historical but rather dogmatic. It is only after faith has passed through both types of criticism that it is truly mediated or that it has become scientific knowledge.[18]

The object of criticism is now the orthodox Christological dogma or religious idea that Jesus Christ is the Son of God, one person with two natures, fully divine and fully human. At issue initially is the *contradiction* inherent in declaring the divine and the human to be *truly united* in a finite human life. This contradiction has plagued Christians throughout the ages, according to Strauss, first manifesting itself in early Christological heresies, which either denied that Jesus Christ was fully God or that he was fully human, and surfacing again in Reformation controversies. As scientific thought developed in modern times, it pressed this contradiction ever more to the fore. In fact, the very concept of a personal transcendent God who through a supernatural act sent his son to earth to become human and save the world was rendered incomprehensible by the emergence of Enlightenment reason. This reason claimed autonomy for itself and for the laws by which the world of nature operated. Enlightened rationalists could conceive of a God as the first premise or perhaps as the designer of the natural laws, and they could conceive of a perfectible human reason; they could not, however, conceive of a God-man except as the expression of the ideal of human perfection. The human Jesus retained meaning for rationalists only as a teacher of, and model for, selfless morality.

Strauss writes that the thought of Kant had intensified and made more complex this general Enlightenment Christological dilemma. In *The Critique of Pure Reason* (1781), Kant challenged the truth of metaphysical knowledge, denying that any knowledge of *supersensible* (and thus divine) reality could be attained. He held that the knower could not extend the categories by which he or she knows sensible phenomena (the categories of understanding, *Verstand*) to what is beyond the finite as sensibly experienced. Thus, not only can those categories not be applied to a "God," but they cannot tell us what things are *in themselves* out there in the world. They are innate, subjective categories that provide the basis for objective, scientific, lawlike truth about the world; they do not, however, offer a basis for absolute metaphysical truth (*Vernunft*). In *The Critique of Practical Reason* (1788) Kant wrote about the importance to humans of an idea of moral perfection and the consequent rationality of assuming that this idea exists in order to guarantee that the mandate of conscience, the universally experienced "ought," not be considered meaningless. This *idea* of the moral perfection of humanity is correlated by Kant with an *idea* of an archetype, a Son of God as a perfect person willing to die for others. Belief in this sort of Son of God as a symbol of the *assumed* reality of the goal of conscience, according to Kant, is rational. However, the belief that one specific person in history was, or even could be, this Son of God is neither rational nor necessary.

The conclusions of *The Life of Jesus* appear to agree with the conclusions of the rationalists and Kant: that Jesus was a good moral person and that Christ is the idea of the perfection of the human species. Nineteenth-century intellectuals would have found nothing new in them if Strauss had not proclaimed them Hegelian. But Hegel had come after Kant and the rationalists and had claimed to be able to comprehend philosophically precisely the *orthodox* Christ, the actual God-man of Christian belief.

In contrast to Kant, Hegel held that knowledge of the absolute is possible. He agreed with Kant's assertion against previous rationalists that the understanding (*Verstand*), with its categories of ordinary empirical science, cannot attain knowledge of the absolute, but he held that true metaphysical reason (*Vernunft*) is capable of reaching such truth. The understanding functions to make clear and exact the differences between finite objects, and thus it is not able to comprehend the infinite or the unity of the infinite and the finite. Another level of reason, which can comprehend contradiction, is able to see beyond what seems to be the mutually exclusive realms of the finite and infinite to the truth that they are necessarily inter-related. This level of true metaphysical reason attains the absolute truth, which Hegel named absolute spirit.

Absolute spirit is infinite consciousness that generates the finite as an essential element of its own life. It is not an illusory meta-physical shape like those criticized by Kant because it is infinite thought or idea becoming *actual* in the finite realm of nature and yet remaining itself in the process. In this process, it moves to sublate, to both negate and preserve (*aufheben*), the finite. Hegel's most famous declaration against Kant is that "what is rational is actual."[19] This declaration was at the heart of the philosophical, political, and the-ological debates that preoccupied the followers of Hegel in the 1830s. To the Hegelian theologians, it seemed to create the conditions for defending Christianity's central claim about the actuality of the God-man in history, because that belief could be shown to have the same content as the philosophy of absolute spirit.

Before turning to Strauss's own interpretation of this Hegelian verification of the truth of orthodox Christology, we need to consider another side of Hegel's philosophical project which is important to *In Defense*. On the one side, Hegel criticized the subjectivism found in philosophers like Kant who separated metaphysical truth as a mere idea, as a mere "ought" to be, from the actual world as we can know it. With Kant's work, Hegel placed Johann Gottlieb Fichte's (1762-1814) philosophy of the self as the source of all truth. On the other side, he criticized philosophers like the early Friedrich Schell-ing (1775-1854), whom he thought identified too readily the actual and the rational. This type of philosopher, represented also by Bar-uch Spinoza (1632-77), lacked a dialectical concept of the relationship between the infinite and the finite, without which the infinite absorbs or destroys the reality of the finite. For example, Hegel condemned Schelling for trying to leap over the standpoint of common rationalism to intuit immediately the infinite in the finite.

To describe this side of Hegel's project another way, common rationalism, with its categories of ordinary empirical science, can see the finite only as distinct and separate from the infinite, because its categories, like those of mathematics, are understood as being fixed opposites. True speculative reason, however, is dialectical and can see that these categories are interrelated. It can see that the infinite is only infinite by being in relation to the finite, and that this relationship is of a type that allows the finite to remain itself and at the same time be one with the universal.

Through a tortuous and lengthy process in *The Phenomenology of Spirit* (1807), Hegel demonstrated that the truth and the model for all knowing is absolute spirit, an infinite that "others" itself in the finite, in nature, and in human consciousness in the very process of becoming itself as self-consciousness. Hegel rejected, therefore, the adequacy of the mathematical model for thought accepted by common rationalism, and he substituted for it a model of life. The mathematical model reduces everything to general and abstract laws, on the one hand, and to individual units, on the other, and it keeps the individual and universal separate. In contrast, the model of life conceives the whole as an organism and thus accounts for an inner purposiveness that holds individuals together without destroying their uniqueness and independence.

Furthermore, self-conscious life, not biological life, was Hegel's model. He wrote that he sought to avoid "the night in which all cows are black,"[20] into which Schelling's philosophy took one. In other words, he rejected a merely intuitive grasp of the unity of the infinite with the finite, which seemed to render the world "alive" with inner purposiveness but in effect dissolved all difference. His model of self-conscious life was not of the isolated self but rather of interpersonal relations, that is, of social life. It is, in a sense, the interplay between self-reflective consciousnesses, subjectivities, that binds the universal and the individual. At its most basic level this interplay is between God as self-reflective subject and humans as self-reflective subjects, God as infinite subjectivity and humans as finite and free. The expression of this model in a religious idea or representation is the incarnation; its philosophical comprehension is absolute truth.

In the conclusion to *The Life of Jesus*, Strauss affirms that Hegel's philosophy can secure the truth of Christian faith, even in the face of the loss of its historical verification, because it can comprehend the contradiction inherent in the image of a unity of the divine and the human. He writes, "Hegelianism says of God that he is a Spirit and of man that he is also a Spirit," and thus "it follows that the two are not essentially distinct." Spirit is constituted by the capability of remaining itself while truly othering itself. Thus "the true and real existence of Spirit, therefore, is neither in God by himself nor in man by himself, but in the God-man; neither in the infinite alone, nor in the finite alone, but in the interchange of impartation and withdrawal between the two, which on the part of God is revelation, on the part of man religion."[21]

Religion plays a role in what is a development of the self-consciousness of absolute spirit in its necessary interrelation with human self-consciousness. In this development, religion functions "as the form in which this truth [of the nature of absolute spirit] presents itself to the popular mind, as a fact obvious to the senses,"[22] as what Hegel called representation. The incarnation of Christ is the perfect religious representation because it presents the truth that God is man, and "man is of a divine race." Strauss describes the verification of the truth of dogma from the truth of speculative reason most directly when he writes, "If God and man are in themselves *one*, and if religion is the human side of this unity, then must this unity be made evident to man in religion, and become in him consciousness and reality."[23]

But there remains one last dilemma: granted that Hegel's philosophy makes conceivable the actual unity of God and humans, does it make conceivable this actual unity in one, single human? As Strauss puts it, "If reality is ascribed to the idea of the unity of the divine and human natures, is this equivalent to the admission that this unity must actually have been once manifested, as it never had been, and never more will be, in one individual? This is indeed not the mode in which Idea realizes itself; it is not wont to lavish all its fullness on one exemplar, and be niggardly towards all others: it rather loves to distribute its riches among a multiplicity of exemplars which reciprocally complete each other."[24]

Strauss then asks the two questions raised over and over again in *In Defense*: "Is not the idea of the unity of the divine and human natures a real one in a far higher sense, when I regard the whole race of mankind as its realization, than when I single out one man as such a realization?" In other words, what is the truly real, the actual? Second, "Is not an incarnation of God from eternity a truer one than an incarnation limited to a particular point of time?"[25]

Strauss answers himself in the famous conclusion to *The Life of Jesus*. Hegelianism rightly understood provides the "key" to the whole of Christology.

"As the subject of the predicate which the Church assigns to Christ, we place, instead of an individual, an idea; but an idea which has an existence in reality, not in the mind only, like that of Kant. In an individual, a God-man, the properties and functions which the Church ascribes to Christ contradict themselves; in the idea of the human species they perfectly agree. Humanity is the union of the two natures—the incarnate God, the infinite Spirit alienated in the finite and the finite Spirit recollecting its infinitude; it is the child of the visible Mother and the invisible Father, Nature and Spirit [a rational virgin birth]; it is the worker of miracles, insofar as in the course of human history the Spirit more and more subjugates nature, both within and around man, until it lies before him as the inert matter on which he exercises his active power."[26]

Even after a storm of protest broke around him and he had been thrown out of the Hegelian school (as well as out of Tübingen, never to be accepted back into a university), Strauss did not change this conclusion. In reasserting it in *In Defense* he proclaims that "the victory that humanity wins by culture over nature within itself and by inventions or machines over nature outside of itself is of more value than any victory over nature won by a mere word of a *Thaumaturgen*" (p. 57).

## *The Structure of "In Defense"*

The *Defense* of the Hegelianism of *The Life of Jesus* is divided into three parts: an explication of how "the general principles of the

Hegelian philosophy do not exclude a critique of the gospel history" (pp. 4-20); a synoptic analysis of Hegel's own opinion of the historical validity of the gospel history (pp. 21-37); and a description and rebuttal of the right and center of the Hegelian theological school (pp. 38-66).

## A Hegelian Critique

In the first part Strauss gives an interpretation of the relation of the Hegelian philosophy to critical philosophy. He argues that *The Phenomenology of Spirit*, the linchpin of Hegel's system, is itself a critique of consciousness, and as such it maintains while surpassing the accomplishment of Kant's *Critique of Pure Reason*. In other words, Strauss argues that Hegel's philosophy, while succeeding in comprehending that the "actual is rational" and thus affirming that the objectively given in religion has an intrinsic meaning that is knowable, does not eliminate the Kantian principle that the knowledge of the finite in its finitude is incommensurate with knowledge of the absolute truth. In fact, asserts Strauss, it is the retention of the value of this critique that distinguishes Hegel's philosophy from Schelling's, which attempts to assert that the knowledge of the absolute is immediately attainable through an intellectual intuition into the finite. It is Schelling's philosophical position, not Hegel's, that can be translated into the theological affirmation that the immediately given in religion, "sacred history and dogma," reveals the absolute, and that the truth in what is believed can be discovered "by a kind of clairvoyance" (p. 12). Clairvoyance is far removed from the ordered and exacting process undertaken on the Hegelian route to truth.

What Strauss does is make the fascinating case that the followers of a type of philosophy like Schelling's are naive positivists in the sense that they absolutize as the truth what is before them as the *fact* and thus affirm "that it is the task of philosophy in its relation to the Christian religion to conceive the biblical (especially the gospel) facts as facts" (p. 12-13). The only way to move beyond the sort of positivism that cripples rather than strengthens belief is to be truly Hegelian and thus to incorporate critique into theology. The Hegelian theologians should refuse to identify the level of fact, the level of the data of sense perception, the "this," with absolute truth. Strauss writes, in Hegel's system "everything that is immediate is drawn into a process of mediation, which leaves it neither in its original form nor in its original value" (p. 13).

In short, Strauss argues that the historical investigation of the gospel narratives is a *rejection* of positivism—not at all an adoption of it, as so many of even his twentieth-century critics have charged. Theirs is a charge not easily sustained in the light of Strauss's brilliant and lucid position in the *Defense*. His defense of Hegelian critique met the theological Hegelians head on and carved out the basic interpretation of Hegel that would be developed by the philosophical left wing.

The theological Hegelians, however, had ready a counter charge to this left-wing stance. They labeled it subjectivist because it failed to acknowledge the "coincidence of truth and actuality" and attempted to talk about the truth in the idea but of a truth "which yet has no historical reality" (p. 14). The idea in question is, of course, that of the God-man, and for the theological Hegelians the coincidence of truth and actuality with regard to this idea meant that its true realization was God's complete appearance in one finite individual, Jesus. To identify the idea of the God-man with the idea of the human species, as Strauss did, was to be a subjectivist.

In answering this charge, Strauss at first considers hypothetical Christological positions that would be able to include a special recognition of Jesus. He acknowledges that Hegel had written that "at the pinnacle of all actions, including world-historical actions, stand individuals as subjectivities realizing the substantial" (p. 15). This could mean that some sort of preeminence, analogous to that accorded to geniuses in history, such as Plato, Shakespeare, and Caesar, could be attributed to Jesus, who was no doubt a religious genius. In other words, at the pinnacle of all human actions stand geniuses, outstanding individuals who as self-conscious humans (subjectivities) realize the underlying potential (substance) of humanity. It might even be said, continues Strauss, that religious genius is a type of genius higher than others because it involves the most intimate unity between God and the human. Furthermore, it is possible that some-one might reach the highest attainment of this highest religious ge-nius and know that he or she is one with God in immediate consciousness (p. 18).

Strauss sketches out a sort of human cone, with the peak rep-resenting what could be called the God-man, one who had attained the highest stage of unity with God and thus a qualitatively distinct human perfection. After constructing a pinnacle on which the in-dividual Jesus might be placed, however, Strauss, with two swift moves, backs away from putting him there (pp. 18-19). First he declares that only historians, not theologians or philosophers laying out the conditions of what is possible, can determine whether Jesus actually had the unity with God that would have given him his place at the pinnacle. Moreover, the *possibility* allowed in Hegelian phi-losophy that someone occupy a pinnacle is not the same as the *necessity* that someone do so. So again it is history, not philosophy, that is the judge. Second, Strauss says that even if solid historical evidence were at hand to prove that Jesus actually was aware and spoke as one with God and thus could be called the God-man, he could not *alone* be identified with the full incarnation of God or with the idea of the God-man. A complete identification would entail Jesus' preem-inence in all the other, admittedly lesser, fields of culture such as art and science. Strauss does not say that the entire cone, not just the pinnacle, is the full incarnation of God. His metaphors change here from those of space to those of time, and he asserts that the incarnation of God is fulfilled throughout history, in a process of temporal development in which nodal points can be discerned but from which none can be lifted singly as an absolute.

With these two moves Strauss backs the theological Hegelians into the very corner into which they wanted to trap him. To grant Jesus the status of God-man, as they had wanted to do, Strauss insists that they would have had to disavow the Hegelian principle of the gradual development of the self-consciousness of the infinite in the history of human culture and to assert that Hegel's philosophy demonstrated *a priori* that a single God-man must come forth in history. But a Hegelian philosophy without the development in history of spirit and with only *a priori* arguments about what must be or ought to be is truly one indistinguishable from that of Kant. It would be blatantly and undeniably subjectivist.

## Hegel's Ambiguity on Jesus as the Christ

A capsule version of the core of Hegel's philosophy of religion—its treatment of the issue of representation and concept in the Christian religion—is presented in the second part of *In Defense*.[27] To be able to appropriate Hegel's philosophy in such a version is a rare and pleasant experience. Certainly, Strauss structured what is essentially a synopsis to serve his argumentative purposes, but even if one rejects his interpretation of Hegel, one has to acknowledge that few of Hegel's disciples could condense his view so adroitly. Moreover, it can be said that Strauss was fair in at least highlighting the ambiguities which every able Hegel scholar admits exist in his treatment of Christianity.

For Hegel, religion is that aspect of human culture corresponding to the stage of the development of absolute spirit in which its identity as self-consciousness is recognized but not yet realized in and for itself, as it is in absolute knowing. This identity is perceived through some sort of finite form—through a representation—such as the Egyptian pyramids, the sun, or the Greek gods. The most perfect form for this recognition of absolute spirit as self-consciousness is, of course, self-consciousness itself, the actual living human being. Christianity understands God in this most perfect form; its representation is completely adequate. Thus it is the absolute religion.

Strauss begins his synopsis by putting forth the contrast between Hegel's explicit affirmation of the centrality and necessity of the incarnation to the attainment of absolute truth and his statements about the inadequacy of the human Jesus to bear the content of this incarnation (pp. 21-23). Hegel wrote, "The incarnation of the divine essence . . . is the simple content of the absolute religion,"[28] which content is the same as that of absolute knowing. He also wrote that if one does no more than see Christ as a human, as a teacher of humanity like Socrates, then one does not share the perspective of the true religion. This entire part of *In Defense* is organized around

Hegel's statements about the two different perspectives or stand-points that can be taken toward Jesus Christ—one that considers him "in and with the spirit" and the other that sees him as an ordinary human, conditioned as anyone else by his environment. Strauss makes a case that Hegel does not conflate the two nor try to deduce the truth of one from the truth of the other, that is, neither the truth of faith (in and with spirit) from the truth of history (historical knowledge of the actual man), nor the truth of history from the truth of faith.

The issue that threatens to muddy the waters between this Christ of faith and this Jesus of history is the philosophical necessity Hegel finds for the particularity, singleness, and immediacy of the manifestation of absolute spirit in the human (pp. 23-24). Hegel did write that the incarnation "appears in Christianity in such a way that it is the belief of the world that spirit is there as one self-consciousness, i.e., as an actual human, that he exists for immediate certainty, that the believing consciousness sees and feels and hears this divinity."[29]

But, asks Strauss, does this mean that a human Jesus had Spirit's self-consciousness for his own such that it could be seen, felt, and heard objectively, or does it mean that it is the belief of the world that he did? Is Hegel deducing the necessity "of the consciousness of the individual *in whom* the unity of God and humanity has become manifest" or rather "the consciousness of those *for whom* that individual was the God-man"(p. 24; emphasis added)? In a search through Hegel's texts for an answer, Strauss cites passages referring to two interrelated themes: the ripeness of the Greco-Roman world for the emergence of the belief that God became man in a single, actual human (pp. 24-25), and the essential role of the death of Jesus in occasioning the belief that he was the God-man (pp. 25-30). He attempts to document that Hegel at least inferred that the human Jesus and the need of the world to believe in an actual God-man came together at a moment in history and that after Jesus' death his followers invested in him from their own corporate consciousness the full content of that belief. The life history of Jesus, then, "from which the occasion accidentally was taken to evoke the idea in itself"

(p. 27), is not qualitatively different from any other human life history.

To reinforce the possibility of this interpretation Strauss appeals to Hegel's statements on the subordinate status of the religious representation in relation to that of the philosophical concept. To reach the concept, which takes the form of "the universal self, of the self that in its immediate actuality is at the same time cancelled, of thinking, of universality, without the self being lost in these."[30] To attain the concept, the immediacy of the representation and its particularity must be sublated. Strauss initially refers to Hegel's description of the two stages of the process of transformation from representation to concept. In the first stage, the God-man is present after the death of Jesus in the consciousness of each believer as a memory of the one, single Christ. In the second stage, each person truly realizes that the incarnation, which belief represents as having happened in a single life, is happening now in himself or herself; thus, he or she realizes that the incarnation "lies implicitly in the essence and concept of humanity" (pp. 27).

Strauss cites further what is perhaps Hegel's most direct statement on the historical validity of the representation of the incarnation: "The question of the truth of the Christian religion immediately divides into two questions: (1) Is it true in general that God does not exist without the Son and that God sent him into the world? and (2) Was this Jesus of Nazareth, the carpenter's son, the Son of God, the Christ?" (pp. 31-32).[31] Strauss shows that Hegel's philosophy answered yes to the first question but that it did not, indeed it could not, answer the second. There is no doubt that Hegel held that historical knowledge could not prove claims of faith; he wrote that "the historical, juridical way of attesting to a fact" could not verify the truths of spirit. One could not go from the knowledge of Jesus as a carpenter's son to the affirmation that he was the Son of God. But did Hegel think that the truths of spirit verify history? Of course, this is the question at issue throughout the *Defense*, and at this point in its development Strauss rests his own case on Hegel's ambiguity. Hegel says things like "the history of Christ is valued not merely as a myth . . . but as something totally historical," and yet he allegorizes the narrative of the virgin birth, casts doubts on some of the miracle stories, and says he cannot find any factual basis for the stories of Jesus' resurrection and ascension (pp. 33-36).

In the face of such contradictory statements, Strauss makes three conclusions about Hegel's view of the gospel history. First, he contends that Hegel believed that the most significant factor in the appearance of faith in Jesus as the God-man was the need of humans at that time to "perceive the unity of the divine and the human in sensible presence." Second, he states that the meaning of the individual gospel stories is "independent of their historical validity," and so Hegel puts no constraints on historical critique. His third point is that Hegel wanted to say that Jesus is unique in relation to the incarnation, but "left in what way and to what extent partly undefined" and partly qualified by the fact that he found the consciousness of the Christian community after the death of Jesus more fulfilled than Jesus' own (p. 37).

## Dividing Right from Left

In this most lively part of the *Defense*, the actual battles between Strauss and his Hegelian critics are reenacted. The turning point of this historical drama is a brilliantly written parody of Bruno Bauer's right-wing theological treatment of the doctrine of the virgin birth. Strauss puts the critique he discussed on theoretical grounds in the first part of *In Defense* into action in this final part. His critique's principal object is, of course, right-wing Hegelian theology, and he uses as a tool the comic devices that are so evident in *The Life of Jesus* itself. Just as the positions of the supernaturalists and rationalists are shown to be ridiculous in *The Life of Jesus*, the right-wing theologians' speculative justification of the historical validity of the Gospels is displayed as the "babble of a thousand fools." Nevertheless, in the *Defense* the comic is restrained, emerging only once between Strauss's seriously and carefully argued responses to the omnipresent accusation that his position was subjectivist. Yet, in this context as in the context of the revered subject matter and ordered procedures of *The Life of Jesus*, the comic is a startling and effective tool of critique.

The backdrop for this concrete engagement between Strauss's

left side of the Hegelian school and the right and center is drawn in the first two parts of *In Defense*, the conclusions of which Strauss rehearses again: Hegel's own lack of clarity concerning the person and life of Jesus, and the dual relation of his philosophy to that of Schelling, which grounds its preservation of a role for critique. Furthermore, Strauss's basic tactic is the same here as in the other parts. He set out to demonstrate that his critics, not he, are the subjectivists, and once again he links subjectivism and positivism.

The overall structure of this section follows party lines. The first and longest section refutes the right wing of the Hegelian school, represented by Carl Göschel, Gabler, and Bruno Bauer (pp. 38-60); the middle and much shorter section deals with the center, occupied by Karl Rosenkranz (pp. 60-66); and the last section is a two-line identification of Strauss as the left wing (p. 66). The content of this part is clear and needs no summary here, but, because of their importance for the on-going debates about the meaning of Hegelianism for philosophy and religion, several of Strauss's elucidations of the meaning of Hegelian critique made in the course of his refutations will be highlighted.

Göschel couched the subjectivist charge against Strauss in strong religious language and set the stage for Strauss's initial, almost passionate, explication of critique. Göschel called historical critique a primal act of human pride which denies the power of the infinite to appear in the finite and thus of God to act in history. To him *The Life of Jesus* was the expression of an egoistic refusal to submit to anything outside the self, anything given to the human self as true. Because of its identification of the God-man as the totality of the human species, a totality which can exist only in thought as the idea of the human species, *The Life of Jesus* was nothing more than Kant's subjectivism revived as "perversion."

Strauss met this accusation with the concise and telling argument that even if one wanted to affirm the orthodox view of Christ as the God-man, the activity of reflective thought would be necessary for one to "comprehend a series of single phenomena" in order to find the total fullness of the divine humanity of Christ. This fullness could not be evident at every isolated moment of his life. So even with an orthodox Christ "the reality of the idea [of the God-man] would be, in the final instance, only a reality in thought" (p.43). The reason Göschel could not understand this, or more to the point, that he could not understand that the actuality of the idea is truly realized in the idea of the human species, is that he is the one who has the Kantian problem. He is "incapable of synthetically comprehending [the idea's] presentation in a mass of separated phenomena which mutually complete each other and form the unity of a true actuality" (p. 43). The result of this subjectivism is "nominalistic dependence on empirical individuality," that is, naive positivism, not the true realism of Hegel (p. 43).

This argumentation is more than a simple statement of the logic of realism. It touched the vital nerve of *The Life of Jesus*, the substitution of human collectivity for an individuality which by definition excluded others. Although Strauss did not expand on the social and political implications of this logic (and more than likely did not himself intend to draw any), other left-wing Hegelians would find it central to their criticism of the state as well as religion.

The second important elucidation of Hegelian critique made by Strauss has to do with its presuppositions. In response to Bauer, who wrote that Strauss's critique could not grasp the true nature of the gospel history because he presupposed from the beginning of his investigation that it was not valid, Strauss affirms that critique ought not to be prejudiced with regard to its results. What Bauer and the other Hegelians of the right sought, however, was a theological critique that would presuppose that it will find its object "absolutely testworthy" (p. 44). But how can there be critique at all if it does not presuppose its possibility and accept its right to find a lack of truth in its object? Why should even the critique of the biblical literature of the absolute religion give up this presupposition? A critique "that presupposes its object to be absolute and without fault is precisely no critique" (p. 46). Here Strauss in effect declares that Hegelian critique guarantees the right to take up any object with a measure of doubt. The left wing soon drew the conclusion that if religion is not exempt from such a critique, neither is the state.

Strauss's parody of Bauer's treatment of the virgin birth comes immediately after his assertion of the rights of critique. Here the comic serves to heighten the freedom that critique assumes. By conjuring up ludicrous images of what could possibly be meant by the rationality and thus actuality of a virginal conception of Jesus by the agency of the Holy Spirit, Strauss drives home another essential point about critique—that it can comprehend contingency in a way that right-wing Hegelian theology cannot. Both the use of the comic and the direct argumentation in this section buttress Strauss's claim that true speculation, and his critique as an element of it, recognize "the inner necessity in precisely the freest play of contingency" (p. 48). The Christian representation of the incarnation, according to Hegel, is adequate to absolute knowing precisely because it brings together absolute necessity and the freest play of contingency. Strauss in effect argues that only critique can comprehend this representation.

The section on the center of the Hegelian school, represented only by Karl Rosenkranz, contains no new explanations of critique. It could almost be described as anticlimactic if it were not that Rosenkranz's position is so close to Hegel's itself that it serves as a repetition of the second part of *In Defense*. Hegel's ambiguity is called to mind in Rosenkranz's admission that parts of the Gospels are not historically valid, that "history cannot be arrested with Jesus as a single being of the past," and yet that Jesus "alone and no other human was adequate to the concept" of the divine and human unity (p. 64). Strauss takes the opportunity presented by this rehearsed ambiguity to repeat his own view that Hegel's philosophy might make conceivable the historical existence of an individual who had attained the goal of religious genius, but that it leaves to historical critique the determination of whether Jesus was this individual.

*In Defense* ends with Strauss telling us that he would take his stand on the left wing of the Hegelian school if it did not want "to exclude me completely from its ranks and to throw me into other intellectual camps—of course, only to catch me when, just like a ball, I was thrown back again" (p. 66). The pathos of this statement was borne out at least in the externals of Strauss's future. Not only did he never receive an academic post, he also almost immediately gave up his own tenuous position on the left wing of the Hegelian school to Feuerbach, who wrote *The Essence of Christianity* in 1841.

The story of *The Life of Jesus* and *In Defense*, then, is not to be found in Strauss's own biography; rather, it is found in the brilliance of their shocking marriage of Hegel's philosophy and an unstinting critique of religion.

## Notes to the Introduction

1. Heinrich Heine, "Concerning the History of Religion and Philosophy in Germany," in *Selected Works*, trans. and ed. Helen M. Mustard (New York: Random House, 1973), p. 276. In its original form this essay appeared in a series of three articles published in France in 1834 in the *Revue des deux mondes*. The following year the articles were collected under the title *Zur Geschichte der Religion und Philosophie in Deutschland* and published by Hoffmann and Campe in Hamburg.

2. David Friedrich Strauss, *Das Leben Jesu, kritisch bearbeitet*, 2 vols. (Tübingen: Osiander, 1835-36). Volume 2 bears the date 1836, but it appeared in October 1835. Volume 1 appeared in June 1835. For the sake of brevity, this title will most often be shortened to *The Life of Jesus*. A second edition appeared in 1837, and the third, significantly altered, appeared in 1838. The fourth edition, which was much like the first, appeared in 1840. George Eliot translated this edition into English in 1846. In 1972, this translation was reprinted by Fortress Press, Philadelphia, with an editorial introduction and notes comparing the four editions by Peter C. Hodgson. Most citations will be to this edition. Where I quote passages from the first edition which are unchanged in the fourth edition, I use Eliot's translation with only minor stylistic revisions. When the passages do not agree, the translations are my own and citations are from the 1835 German edition.

3. For descriptions of the impact of *The Life of Jesus*, see the two recent biographies of Strauss: Horton Harris, *David Friedrich Strauss and His Theology* (Cambridge: Cambridge University Press,

1973), and Richard S. Cromwell, *David Friedrich Strauss and His Place in Modern Thought* (Fair Lawn, N.J.: R. E. Burdick, Inc., 1974).

4. This description was given by Ferdinand Christian Baur in a letter to a friend written in October 1836. The letter appears in the *Preussische Jahrbücher* 160:483-85. A portion of the letter is translated in Harris, *David Friedrich Strauss and His Theology*, pp. 86-88.

5. David Friedrich Strauss, *Streitschriften zur Vertheidigung meiner Schrift über das Leben Jesu und zur Charakteristik der gegenwärtigen Theologie*, 3 parts (Tübingen: Osiander, 1837). Strauss's defense appears in the third part of his polemical writings (pp. 55-126). It is given the title of the Hegelian journal *Jahrbücher für wissenschaftliche Kritik*, in which the criticism of *The Life of Jesus* appeared. Strauss also responds in part three to the criticisms appearing in the conservative, theologically orthodox journal *Die evangelische Kirchenzeitung* and the liberal *Theologische Studien und Kritiken*. In the first part of the *Polemical Writings*, Strauss discusses the theology of one of his own Tübingen professors, J. C. F. Steudal (1779-1831) under the title "The Self-Deception of Present-day Rational Supernaturalism." In the second part he discusses another professor, C. A. Eschenmayer (1768-1852), and the most famous literary critic of the day, Wolfgang Menzel (1798-1873). In this introduction, citations to *In Defense of My "Life of Jesus"* will be by page number and placed in parentheses in the text. The title will be given as *In Defense* or simply *Defense*.

6. See Marilyn Chapin Massey, *Christ Unmasked: The Meaning of "The Life of Jesus" in German Politics* (Chapel Hill, N.C.: University of North Carolina Press, 1983) for a discussion of the political role of *The Life of Jesus* in the period before the revolution of 1848.

7. Karl Marx, "Zur Kritik der Hegelischen Rechts-Philosophie: Einleitung," in *Deutsch-Französische Jahrbücher*, ed. Karl Marx and Arnold Ruge (Paris: Bureau der Jahrbücher, 1844), p. 71.

8. For a discussion of this request and Göschel's response, see Walter Jaeschke, "Urmenschheit und Monarchie: Eine politische Christologie der Hegelschen Rechten," *Hegel-Studien*, ed. Friedhelm Nicolin and Otto Pöggeler, vol. 14 (Bonn: Bouvier Verlag Herbert Grundmann, 1979).

9. Strauss, *The Life of Jesus*, p. 130.

10. Ibid., pp. 119-21.

11. Ibid., p. 123.

12. Ibid., p. 130.

13. Ibid., p. 138.

14. Ibid., p. 140.

15. Ibid.

16. The Hegelian issue, of course, is whether "imagined" history is truly objective.

17. Strauss, *Das Leben Jesus*, 2:736.

18. Strauss, *The Life of Jesus*, p. 7-58. (Emphasis added)

19. See G. W. F. Hegel, *Enzyklopädie der philosophischen Wissenschaften im Grundrisse*, ed. F. Nicolin and O. Pöggeler (Hamburg: Felix Meiner, 1959), no. 6.

20. G. W. F. Hegel, *The Phenomenology of Mind*, trans. J. G. Baillie (New York: Harper and Row, 1967), p. 79.

21. Strauss, *The Life of Jesus*, p. 777.

22. Ibid., p. 778.

23. Ibid., p. 777.

24. Ibid., pp. 779-80.

25. Ibid., p. 780.

26. Ibid.

27. Most of the passages Strauss cites are from Hegel's *Phenomenology* and lectures on the philosophy of religion. Hegel lectured on religion at Berlin in the summer semesters of 1821, 1824, 1827, and 1831. These lectures appeared as Volumes 11 and 12 of G. W. F. Hegel, *Werke: Vollständige Ausgabe durch einen Verein von Freunden des Verewigten*, 18 vols. (Berlin: Duncker and Humbolt, 1832-45). A translation of the third part of these lectures, *The Revelatory, Consummate, Absolute Religion*, has been done by Peter C. Hodgson as *The Christian Religion*, American Academy of Religion Texts and Translations, ed. James A. Massey, no. 2 (Missoula, Mont.: Scholars Press, 1979). Hodgson's discussion of the state of the German texts of these lectures (pp. vii-xxi) is excellent. Strauss referred to the first edition of the lectures (1831), which was edited by Philip Marheineke. This edition differs from the one translated by Hodgson.

Bearing this in mind, however, those interested in looking more closely at Strauss's interpretation of Hegel should look at *Phenomenology*, pp. 750-70, 780-85, and *The Christian Religion*, pp. 169-221, 231-56.

28. See Hegel, *Phenomenology*, p. 758.
29. See ibid., p. 757.
30. See ibid., p. 762.
31. See Hegel, *The Christian Religion*, p. 240.

# IN DEFENSE OF MY
# *Life of Jesus*

# I

# THE GENERAL RELATION OF THE HEGELIAN
# PHILOSOPHY TO THEOLOGICAL CRITIQUE

From the beginning, my critique of the life of Jesus was closely tied to the Hegelian philosophy. In my years at the university, my friends and I thought that the point of Hegel's system most relevant for theology was his distinction in religion between representation and concept, which, although different in form, could still have the same content. In this distinction we found respect for the biblical documents and church dogmas reconciled as nowhere else with the freedom to reflect on them. In a short time, the most important question about this for us became how the concept related to the historical components of the Bible, especially the Gospels: whether the historical character belongs to the content, which since it is the same for both representation and concept, thus demands recognition by the latter; or whether the historical character is to be considered as mere form to which conceptual thought, therefore, is not bound?

Whenever we looked for clarification in the writings of Hegel and his leading disciples, just at the point on which we most wanted light we found ourselves to the greatest extent left in the dark. In Hegel, especially in his *Phenomenology*, the total ambiguity of the concept *Aufhebung*[1]—sublation—revealed itself at this exact point. In one place, history appeared [to]* be dropped away passively as

*Numbers in the margins refer to the pages in the original edition of the *Streitschriften* (1837). Brackets parallel to the numbers enclose the first word on these pages.
[1][The ambiguity of the term *Aufhebung* can be kept in mind if the reader thinks of sublation as a cancellation, as the act of putting a mark across something, say a stamp or a number, without totally obliterating it, in order to attain something. For example, a stamp operates to move mail only when it is canceled. A number in a mathematical calculation may not yield its value until canceled. There is no doubt that for Hegel cancellation of modes or stages of knowing are necessary in the process of attaining true knowledge. The ambiguity arises over the original status of that which is nec-

merely represented when face to face with the completed concept of
the matter. At another place, the historical appeared to be held firmly
together with the idea. It was not clear whether the gospelfact—except
certainly not as an isolated fact but together with the entire world-
historical series of realizations of the idea—should be accepted as the
truth, or whether the concentration of the idea into this one single fact
should be understood as merely an abbreviation for the representing
consciousness. We thought that we detected somewhat more decisive-
ness on this matter from Philip Marheineke. In his interpretation any
negative aspect of the relation of the concept to the historical seemed
almost to disappear behind the affirmative. Indeed, we saw that Carl
Göschel and the entire theological section of the Hegelian school was
striking out more and more in this direction.

But just this direction least satisfied us. We asked ourselves,
"Why make the distinction in religion between representation and
concept if they are not really different, if every time we stay obliged
to the concept, we also find ourselves obliged to the representation?
It is only an illusion of freedom with which we are dazzled if we
are led beyond the fact to the idea only in order to be turned back
again from the idea to the fact. By this method we do not take a
single step forward. Instead, we have spent an enormous amount of
energy just to stay at the standpoint of orthodoxy. Certainly, the
representation, and more precisely, the history, that we secure by
this method present themselves as reborn out of the concept. But
this rebirth becomes dubious because nothing at all is changed in
representation and history. They have kept the identical shape that
they had in the old ecclesiastical system." Because of these questions
we inevitably suspected that representation and history in fact remained unmoved in their original positions and that the apparent
passage through thought had been only a deception.

So, as we struggled to clarify the general relation between religious representation and concept, my friends and I began to think
of writing our own dogmatic. Ours was not going to be like Marheineke's. In his dogmatic only the uppermost layer of fat [was]

essarily canceled. Is that original status preserved in all its worth or is it reduced to
a matter of indifference once the process has moved to a new level?]

being skimmed from the dialectical kettle in which ecclesiastical dogma was stewing. In our kettle all the ingredients would be exposed right from the start and the entire process undertaken before our eyes.

We planned to display first the biblical representations, and after that, how, through their encounter with the one-sided character of heresies, these moved on to be defined as ecclesiastical dogmas. Next we were going to show how this dogma dissolved itself forthwith in the polemic with deism and rationalism in order to reconstitute itself as purified by the concept. According to our schema, then, the content of Christian faith had to pass first through heresy and then through the modern Enlightenment. We felt that Marheineke had neglected especially the latter of these two negative trials. For him dogma appeared to go directly from its ecclesiastical wording into the concept as if its original formulation had merely to be confirmed.

Because of the particular importance that the distinction between representation and concept seemed to have for the gospel history, however, I soon thought of beginning by working through the life of Jesus with this method. According to my original plan, which I outlined during a stay in Berlin, the work—at first intended to be lectures— would have had three parts. The first, the positive or traditional part, would have contained an objective presentation of the life of Jesus according to the evangelists, next, a presentation of the way in which Jesus lives in the subjective hearts of believers, and, finally, the mediation of these two sides in the second article of the Apostles' Creed. The second, the negative or critical part, would have broken up most of the life history of Jesus by questioning its historical truth, while the third part would have reestablished dogmatically that which had been negated. I thought of the title, "The Life of Jesus," along with this original plan. No one can say that this name was not appropriate for such a project. In the course of my work, the projected first part was dropped and the third became nothing but an appendix. The second grew into the actual body of the book. As usually happens in such cases, I did [not] want to give up the original name. I thought that I could make it fit my

60

revised plan by the addition of the phrase, "critically examined." I
want to explain this to show how unjust and precipitous Professors
Ullmann and Tholuck[2] are to say that I chose my title because I
wanted to win a large audience, indeed only out of promotional
speculation.

I had already conceived my original plan in Berlin when I had
the opportunity to obtain two faithful copies of Schleiermacher's
lectures on the life of Jesus which he had given in two different
years.[3] I am going to discuss these lectures for a moment because
the author of the review of my book in the Büchner *Literarischezeitung*
[*Literary Journal*],[4] as well as Professor Karl Rosenkranz,[5] have sur-
mised that I might well be deeply indebted to these lectures for even
the details of my work. The truth is I found myself repelled by
almost every aspect of these lectures. I owe to this aversion to
Schleiermacher's perspective my ability to delineate more clearly my
own view on many parts of the life of Jesus. For example, Schleiermacher proceeded from a construction of the person of Christ out
of the Christian consciousness; this could only impress me as an
uncritical presupposition. Throughout his investigations, he gave
special preference to the fourth Gospel; this had to appear to me for
the time being as an unwarranted bias. In his interpretation of the
most striking occurrences in the life of Jesus, such as the transfig-
uration, resurrection, and events of this sort, he agreed either openly

---

[2][Karl Ullmann (1796-1869) was a so-called liberal theologian who followed the tradition of Friedrich Schleiermacher in seeking to reconcile reason and religion while
insisting, contrary to Hegel, that they were rooted in separate human faculties.
Ullman reviewed Strauss's *The Life of Jesus* in *Theologische Studien und Kritiken* 9 (1836):
770-816. Friedrich August Gottreu Tholuck (1799-1877) was a leading pietist theologian who criticized Strauss in *Über die Glaubwürdigkeit der evangelischer Geschichte,
zugleich eine Kritik des Lebens Jesu von Strauss, für theologische und nicht theologische Leser
dargestellt* (Hamburg: Perthes, 1836).]
[3][Schleiermacher lectured on the life of Jesus five times between 1819 and 1832. These
lectures were not published until 1864. An English translation by S. MacLean Gil-
mour, edited by Jack C. Verheyden and entitled *The Life of Jesus*, was published in
1975 by Fortress Press in Philadelphia.]
[4][The reference here is to the *Literarische Zeitung* (Berlin: Duncker and Humbolt, 1834-
49), edited by Karl Büchner (1806-37), a politically radical dramatist.]
[5][Karl Rosenkranz reviewed *The Life of Jesus* in the introduction to *Kritik der Schleiermacherschen Glaubenslehre* (Königsberg: Gebrüder Bornträger, 1836).]

or implicitly with Dr. H. E. G. Paulus;[6] this was a standpoint I thought I could prove untenable.

After my return from Berlin to Tübingen University, I immediately began giving philosophical lectures. I soon discontinued these, however, to devote myself exclusively to my theological plan. At first I studied and took excerpts from what seemed to be relevant among the older and newer literature—from Celsus to the Wolfenbüttel [fragmentist], from Augustine's harmony of the Gospels up to those of Olshausen and Paulus, and then from the more recent investigations of the authenticity and origin of the Gospels from Eichhorn to Bretschneider and Sieffert.[7] It was from these extensive excerpts that I developed my book. I did not compose it "without any scholarly preparation," as the *Evangelische Kirchenzeitung* [*Evangelical Church Journal*] charged. Somehow that journal had the good will to find this possible, notwithstanding, as it acknowledged, the "scholarly appearance" of my work. Because of these preparatory studies, the second, critical part of my plan gained more and more breadth. It became clear that what I had intended as the first part had to be joined on the one hand to the second and on the other hand to the third. A synopsis of the individual gospel narratives had to precede each time their critique, and the second article of the Apostles' Creed had to be joined to the concluding dogmatic essay. This is how the work in its present shape arose.

I was not surprised that when my book appeared the many opponents of the Hegelian philosophy used its conclusions to demonstrate the destructive consequences of the Hegelian method of philosophizing. I also anticipated the move of the Hegelian school to reject the point of view of my book and protect itself from being identified with it. In a certain sense, both parties are in the right.

Above all, the Hegelians are right when they protest: "is is not our opinion." In fact, it is not. They live in the good faith that

61

---

[6][Paulus wrote his own life of Jesus in 1828, in which he tried to demonstrate how all the gospel narratives can be accepted as historical and still be interpreted to agree with reason.]

[7][Along with Celsus and Augustine, Strauss refers here to the Wolfenbüttel fragmentist, Hermann Samuel Reimarus, and the biblical scholars Hermann Olshausen (1796-1839), Karl G. Bretschneider (1776-1848), and Friedrich Ludwig Sieffert (1803-77).]

when they have identified an idea in a gospel narrative, its historical truth is thereby demonstrated. And when they appeal to Hegel himself and protest that he would not have recognized my book as an expression of his own feelings, I agree. Hegel was personally no friend of historical critique. It annoyed him, as it annoyed Goethe, [to] see the heroic figures of antiquity, to which their higher feeling clung lovingly, gnawed at by critical doubt. If, occasionally, these figures were puffs of mist which they took to be pieces of rock, they did not want to know; they did not want to be disturbed in the illusion by which they felt exalted. This was the cause of Hegel's adverse and clearly unjust judgment of the critical historian Niebuhr[8] and of his frequent expressions of antipathy against the latter's research.

Even apart from Hegel's personal aversion to historical critique, the Hegelian system has a side which critique had to disturb. This is found in its relation to the category of time and to the philosophical systems which immediately preceded it. As the direct development of the principle discovered by Schelling, the Hegelian system opposes the criticism and subjective idealism of Kant and Fichte, which are related negatively and critically to the objectively given in religion as well as in ethics. Hegel's system opposes these idealisms with a character that is more positive and more accepting of the *status quo*— the system of restoration versus the system of revolution. While the Fichtean "I" took reality standing over against it to be a dead mass into which the subject had to import form and understanding through its own activity, Hegel showed the same reality (in the state and religion as well as in nature) as a totality already organized and inspirited on its own. The philosophical systems immediately preceding Hegel's knew only the tautological proposition—"the rational is rational; the actual is actual." They could unite both sides only in the form—"the rational also should be actual; the actual also should be rational." (This, however, is in fact the same as saying that the actual and rational are not truly united.) In contrast, Hegel worked out the propositions that the actual is rational and the rational is actual. The Hegelian term "objective spirit" designates this reversal;

---

[8][Barthold G. Niebuhr (1776-1831) was a noted classical historian.]

that the term jars us even today shows that we still have not entirely broken the habit of the subjective standpoint.

From the perspective of the objective element in the Hegelian philosophy, moreover, critique seems to belong to this outdated subjective standpoint, especially when it is directed against the religious [tradition]. Just as we no longer accept Descartes's theory of animals as machines or Kant's view that purpose in organisms is a rationality merely imported by the subject into nature, we no longer consider popular religions as outgrowths of madness and trickery. We are even beyond considering the Christian religion as one in which the best element is "perfectibility" and as one which is to be the first to be led back through a "censorship" of the thinking subject into "the limits of reason" and purified as a "religion of the mature and of the more perfect." Rationality and truth exist in all reality in general, and thus particularly in religion, the highest spiritual reality, and, in the deepest sense, in the Christian religion as the absolute religion. A critique which makes a move to excise a mass of untruths and unhistorical assertions in Christianity draws from the beginning the accusation that it has not yet been raised to the Hegelian point of view.

Nevertheless, it is not fully accurate or complete to speak of the Hegelian system as simply opposed to the systems of Kant and Fichte. It forms just as much of a contrast to Schelling's system. This latter contrast is not as noticeable as the former, not so much because that contrast is less sharp, but because Schelling's own system is less developed than Kant's and Fichte's. Hegel departs from Kant and Fichte in principle, method, and conclusion; he agrees with Schelling in principle, departs from him in method and, in fact, agrees in part with his conclusions. The contrast of Hegel's system with Schelling's, however, is not as frequently apparent as that with Kant's and Fichte's simply because Schelling did not develop his principle as much or apply it as broadly, especially in the spiritual realm, as did they and Hegel. Thus, particularly in the later and most famous works of Hegel, which belong to the so-called applied parts of his philosophy (the philosophies of right and of religion and most of the *Encyclopedia*), the differences [with] Schelling are not as noticeable as those with the two previous systems, especially with Kant's. Even the *Logic*, although belonging to the pure science of thinking and principally concerned with method, which is the main point of difference between Schelling and Hegel, does not make this contrast evident. The *Logic* is so absorbed in the matter itself that it develops the proper method out of the object, not out of previous erroneous methods. Thus the opposition to Schelling's mode of philosophizing, which permeates the entire work, seldom attains direct expression. It is most explicit in the *Phenomenology*, the work in which Hegel for the first time renounced the banner of Schelling and came forward as a philosopher on his own. The important detailed preface of this book revolves almost completely around Hegel's divergence from Schelling, which is summarized in three slogans: (1) The absolute was created in Schelling's philosophy as if shot from a pistol; (2) It is only the night in which all cows are pure black; (3) Its development into a system is like the procedure of a painter who has on his palette only two colors, red and green, in order to paint a plain with the latter and a historical piece with the former, when what was required was a landscape. The first reproach is related to Schelling's mode of attaining the idea of the absolute, that is, immediately, by intellectual intuition. In the *Phenomenology* Hegel turned this leap into an ordered processive movement. The second reproach relates to his mode of thinking and expressing the idea of the absolute once it has been attained only as the absence of all finite distinctions and not just as much as the imminent positing of a system of distinctions within itself. Hegel gave this development in the *Logic*. The third reprimand concerns the performance of the system with regard to its natural and spiritual content. On this point Hegel's *Encyclopedia*, the philosophies of right and religion, and so on, are apposite. In them, rather than applying in a merely external manner a finished schema to objects as did Schelling, Hegel tried to allow the subject to unfold and distinguish itself out of itself.

65     [In] this opposition of his system to Schelling's, especially in that point of contrast which is designated by the *Phenomenology*, Hegel's system moves in the direction of critique. What was excluded

by Schelling is again taken up by Hegel: the entire *Phenomenology* is a critique of consciousness.[9] But if critique plays a principal role in philosophy as such, it should not be lacking in the application of philosophy to theology. Whereas Schelling's absolute is an immediate, primary reality, and intuition (although an intellectual intuition), for Hegel immediate intuition, from which knowing starts out, is far from being an absolute or ultimate truth. Instead, immediate intuition is a subordinate reality which, by means of a series of mediations in which intuition sublates itself as the truth, there is an ascension to the absolute. Just as sense certainty, along with its object and content, sensible objectivity, is the starting point for knowing in general, believing certainty and its object, the religious tradition as dogma and sacred history, is the starting point for theological knowledge. Progress from the starting point must be the same for theology as for philosophy; progress is a negative mediation, lowering the starting point to the status of a subordinate reality which is not truth on its own grounds. Between dogma in its ecclesiastical expression and sacred history in its biblical appearance, on the one hand, and the true concept in and for itself, on the other, there enters an entire theological phenomenology. In it the beginnings of the religious consciousness cannot fare any better than sense certainty in the philosophical phenomenology. Whoever does not recognize this, whoever conducts only an affirmative mediation between the point of departure and the endpoint, whoever by a kind of intellectual intuition wants to see immediately the absolute truth in the gospel history as such denies the *Phenomenology* in the realm of theology.

If the Hegelian school, in order to characterize my relation to it, adopts the formula—Strauss has fallen back from the Hegelian standpoint to that of Schleiermacher[10]—I think that I can prove, on the contrary, that in theology the Hegelian school has sunk back from the Master's standpoint to Schelling's. For the denial of the *Phenomenology* is the most decisive mark of Schelling's standpoint.

---

[9]On this subject see G. A. Gabler in the review of Julius Schaller's *Die Philosophie unserer Zeit, zur Apologie und Erläuterung des Hegel'schen Systems* (Leipzig: J. C. Hinrichs, 1837) in *Jahrbücher für wissenschaftliche Kritik* (April, 1837), no. 71ff. [Hereinafter cited as *JWK*.]

[10]Rosenkranz, *Kritik*, p. xvii.

In fact, since Hegelians and Schellingians have argued so often about philosophical issues, it is amazing that they relate so peaceably to one another in the theological field. Indeed, until now, partly because of what was said by Hegel, and partly because of what his individual students have been allowed to say, the most beautiful unanimity between the two schools on theology seems to have been the rule. Certainly, in his published writings from his earlier period, Schelling assumed a free attitude to dogma and the biblical history. For example, he maintained that the doctrine that God once became human at a definite point in time and space was nonsense, and he insisted that the incarnation of God be conceived as an eternal process. He thought that much of the gospel history was Jewish fables, which were invented from the Messianic prophecies of the Old Testament; altogether he declared that the first realization of the idea of Christianity in the New Testament was incomplete. Simply, he thought that the idea was not to be found in these books.[11]

This view was not consistent with Schelling's standpoint; it probably did not originate with it. More likely he took it over from Fichte and gave it a new coloring of his own. Since from the Schellingian perspective, the absolute is a philosophical immediate, it follows that the immediately given must also be an absolute for it theologically. In philosophy Schelling's standpoint does not transcend intuition as something incommensurate with attaining the idea. Instead, it raises the intuition itself to intellectual reality. As a consequence, philosophy must not take a step above and beyond sacred history and dogma in order to find the truth. Rather it must discover, by a kind of clairvoyance, the truth in what is believed. In other words, it must discover to be the truth that which is believed itself, without distinguishing its content from the form inadequate to it. Thus, it can only appear to be an application of Schelling's standpoint, which is more consistent than the ones found in his early writings, when one reads now in the writings of his school that it is the task of philosophy in its relation to the Christian religion to

---

[11]Friedrich Schelling, *Vorlesungen über die Methode des academischen Studiums*, 3rd ed. (Stuttgart and Tübingen: J. G. Cotta, 1830). [This work was originally published in 1803.]

conceive the biblical (especially the gospel) facts as facts.[12] It also sounds more consistent when one hears Schelling himself say that in theological matters the principal change in his system is that he now attaches it more closely than before to that which is given in the Bible and ecclesiastical dogma.

As I have just said, this view of the relation of philosophy to the Bible and dogma is totally consistent from Schelling's standpoint, but I do not see what it could mean for Hegel's. In his system everything that is immediate is drawn into a process of mediation, which leaves it neither in its original form nor in its original value. At the end of the *Phenomenology* we do not read that we have returned to our beginning sense certainty by a long and devious route. We do not read that we have come to know that sense certainty is the highest form of knowledge, in which the entire spiritual realm is conceived. How, therefore, can the process of speculative [theology] end by stating that the certainty of the believer is the highest form of knowing in which all truth is contained? It cannot. Sense certainty (the "this" and the act of pointing to something) is demonstrated in the process of the *Phenomenology* to be the poorest and emptiest mode of knowing, and thus, believing certainty, the retaining of the indicated "this," "this" miracle, "this" person, in general "this" excision from the rest of history and reality, must be recognized to be a relatively lacking form of a religious life. Just as the "here" is sublated in another "here," the "now" in another "now," and both become universal, so "this" one event is sublated in another event until it is recognized as a universal event.

I do not mean to say that the question of whether or not what the evangelists report actually happened can be decided from the standpoint of a philosophy of religion. What can be decided is the question of whether or not what they report must have happened because of the truth of certain concepts. And my opinin is that, first of all, from the general position of the Hegelian philosophy, the

68

---

[12][Strauss refers here to a statement made by the conservative political philosopher Friedrich Julius Stahl (1802-61) that philosophy will reach a point from which it will be able to accept as true everything in the Gospels.] See Friedrich Julius Stahl, *Philosophie des Rechts nach geschichtlicher Ansicht*, 2 vols. in 3 (Heidelberg: J. C. Mohr, 1830-37), 1:362.

necessity of such an existence of events does not follow in any way.
On the contrary, Hegel's position reduces this history, from which
a beginning is made just as it is from an immediate reality in philosophy, into something indifferent. It reduces it to something which
*could* have happened in such a way but just as well need not. The
decision concerning historical accuracy is peacefully left to the judgment of historical critique. It is the orthodox standpoint which states
that the Christian truth found in the birth or resurrection of Jesus
would not be true if Jesus had not really been conceived in this way
or if he had not actually risen. What advantage does the philosophical
standpoint have over orthodoxy if it in the same way assures us that
as certainly as these truths are true these events must actually have
transpired? This assertion obviously implies the converse, that if the
events did not take place, the truths would not be true.

Even in the face of this import, my Hegelian critics attack me
on precisely this issue, saying: Whoever fails to recognize this coincidence of truth and actuality, whoever still speaks of a truth in
the idea which [yet] has no historical reality, falls back from the
Hegelian standpoint to the Schleiermacherian or the Kantian, that
is, from the standpoint of absolute knowing to that of subjective
thinking. I had to be prepared for this objection from the beginning
of my work. Therefore, I answered it in the conclusion of *The Life
of Jesus* in such a way that I now cannot add anything essential. In
my opinion, the reason for this objection from my Hegelian critics
is their confusion between actuality in general and this particular
actuality. Granted, for example, the ideas of beauty and virtue must
have reality. But can I ever derive out of this truth alone the conclusion that this or that particular human must be beautiful or virtuous? Can someone who refuses to agree that a particular human
being is beautiful or virtuous, or more precisely, is the highest and
only perfect realization of the idea of beauty or of virtue, be justly
accused of denying the entire reality of these ideas?

Deriving from the fact that God both exists and yet does not
exist at this time, in this place, and in this human individual, there
are two sides inhering in the concept of the process of the incarnation
of God. Anyone who stresses only the side of not-yet-being, that

is, of the ought, certainly could be justly accused of sinking back to the Kantian standpoint. But anyone who forgets the side of the ought is also guilty, in this case of a fanciful pantheism in so far as he thinks of humanity as the existing God. But if anyone thinks of one human exclusively as God, then he could perhaps present historical proof. If, however, he rests his case philosophically, he is guilty of the confusion indicated above.

At this point, however, my Hegelian critics respond: The concept of the divine idea includes in itself not merely a realization of God in the self-replenishing totality of individuals but also its complete appearance in one individual. Only this appearance can be called a true realization of the idea. Rosenkranz states: "I see [Strauss's] basic error in the fact that he wishes to assert the subjectivity of substance only in the infinite multiplicity of subjects, in the species of humanity. But the essence of the idea also includes in itself exactly the absoluteness of its appearance as individual, as the single human."[13] Professor Hoffmann, following his tactic of using Hegel against me, which I mentioned before, remarks that my "view of the eternal oscillation of the idea in the individual actually does not allow the recognition of any realization of the idea. Never and nowhere does this reality become perceptible in one, particular individual; instead it exists only in the idea of humanity, in an idea that itself has no limits, in an indeterminate idea. Is the actuality of the idea to be found here?"[14]

70

I can see the point of this criticism. Hegel's statement that "at the pinnacle of all actions, including world-historical actions, stand individuals as subjectivities realizing the substantial"[15] can be extended to mean that in general all the various tendencies in which the realm of divine life is articulated in humanity are represented by great individuals. Of course, then, a few individuals are separated

---

[13]Rosenkranz, *Kritik*, p. xvii. See G. A. Gabler, *De Verae philosophiae erga religionem christianam pietate* (Berlin: Duncker and Humblot, 1836), p. 42.
[14]Wilhelm Hoffmann, *Des Leben Jesu, kritisch bearbeitet von Dr. D.F. Strauss. Geprüft für Theologen und Nichttheologen* (Stuttgart: P. Balz, 1836), p. 435.
[15]G. W. F. Hegel, *Grundlinien der Philosophie des Rechts* (Berlin: Nicolai, 1821), para. 348, p. 433.

out of the mass of the totality as preeminent bearers of the divine life. But this sort of preeminence still implies a plurality in two respects. First, the spheres or departments, so to speak, into which the life of humanity is divided in being an expression of the divine are plural—the practical life is distinguished from the life of theory, religion is distinguished from science and art. And within these fields there are divisions; for example, art is distinguished from science. Thus, war heroes and statesmen, religious founders and philosophers, painters and poets, [and] so forth, flash by quickly and we catch a glimpse of sides of the divine life in each of them. Second, even within each sphere, all its content and energy are not concentrated in one individual, but a Caesar follows an Alexander and a Solon follows a Lycurgus. Philosophy was not exhausted in the great figure of Socrates; it also produced a Plato, an Aristotle, a Spinoza. In the same way, poetry did not end with Homer or Aeschylus, but, on the contrary, it has always found new embodiments in a series of individuals which leads up to Shakespeare and the latest poets.

Concerning the first mode of plurality, it would seem that a single area of human life would be unjust to all the others if it inscribed inside of itself exclusively an incarnation of God. Such incarnations of God are real in every area of human life according to its own mode. Immediately, it must be said that the various areas in which humanity is capable of manifesting the divine in itself are not simply equal types. At the same time, they can be distinguished as stages, and one stage can be called the highest because the incarnation of God can be said to be in it in a sense in which it is in no other. But this distinction in the grade of the various spheres of higher and higher human activities will not solve the problem of plurality because, more carefully considered, there is no reason why a Phidias should be put above or below a Raphael, or both related in such a manner to a Sophocles or a Shakespeare, or Shakespeare to a Plato and a Spinoza, or all these taken together to a Caesar or a Napoleon. It can be said of these individuals that one attained more or less and presented humanity more or less purely in his own sphere than another did in his. But these individuals cannot be ranked according to a distinction in the value of the areas themselves. So the desired hierarchy of the various areas of life is transformed into a circle in which they all lie in different directions, but at an equal distance, around the common axis. And they [receive] equally strong impulses from the common source.          72

Only one area of human life seems to resist this arrangement—religion. It will not at all let itself be placed on a scale with the rest or with them on the periphery of the circle. Religion, rather, makes a claim to place itself at the middle point of the circle, closest to the divine source. A Moses, even a Muhammad, can be compared as lawgivers and military leaders to Solon and Alexander. As religious founders, however, they have the advantage over the latter, and they have something that not only belongs to another area of life but to a definitely higher one. While all the other heroes of our species find and present the divine indirectly (in peoples and stages, ideas or songs, shapes, colors, or tones), a religious genius—if I can use this expression here—draws near the divine essence as such and immediately presents its relation to the human spirit. In the genius, the threads of this relation, which are later apportioned to the various other human tendencies, are still all together. Therefore, it can be said that in no other realm is the divine essence so immediately, concentratedly, and energetically realized than in the religious realm. Indeed, an incarnation of God can be expressed by no other realm in the same sense as this one.

But here the second aspect of the problem of pluralism discussed above comes into question. Even presupposing the religious realm as, in the highest sense, that of the incarnation of God, still, the divine life imparted within a single sphere is not exhausted in one great individual but is presented in a series of them. Members in this series can be ranked in an ascending order but not so that anyone ever presents a decisive *non plus ultra*. Thus, Moses and the prophets in relation to Christ constitute an ascending series just like that of earlier poets to Shakespeare. But no individual in the religious series nor any in the poetic [can] be placed on an exclusive pinnacle beyond          73 which it is impossible to rise. It is noteworthy that in the religious field great individuals are much more rare and that the periods between their appearance are far longer than for those outstanding individuals in any other field. Great military heroes and statesmen, as well as artists and philosophers, appear after far shorter intervals than the great figures who serve as reference points for the religious life of people. Especially from the time of Christ until the present, the productivity in religion seems to have been totally exhausted. Since the foundation of Christianity, the field has produced only afterbirths, such as Islam. Nevertheless, to rest a claim for the insuperability of Christ on this type of certainty would be precarious. Christ would have merely a comparatively highest rank, because, on the one hand, he could be differentiated only by degree from all the other great persons and, on the other, it would always remain uncertain whether, even after such a long interval, someone else would still transcend him.

This perspective on the relative dignity of Christ is altered by the following line of argument. Since (1) the incarnation of God is the progressive realization of the unity of the divine and human natures, and (2) religion is the sphere of the innermost and highest form of this unification (i.e., in the immediate human self-consciousness), then the highest possible attainment in the religious sphere would be that a human knows himself in his immediate consciousness to be one with God. And, insofar as the religious is the highest sphere, this is the highest human attainment of all. No one can transcend this point because it is the very attainment of the goal. The points lying below this goal (such as reached by Moses and the prophets), which approximate the unification of the divine and human consciousness, stand in a quantitative relation to it. Yet these are also qualitatively distinct from it, just as distinct as nonunity is from unity. Whether this unification of the divine and human nature actually took place in Christ can be decided only by historians, not philosophers. Even that such a human ever must come forth in history cannot be demonstrated *a priori*. At all events, the proposition—"The essence of the idea also includes in itself exactly the

absoluteness of its appearance as individual, [as] this single human"— 74
is only propounded by the Hegelian school, not proven.

What if the new wave of historical-critical research, especially
that on the origin and character of the fourth Gospel, demonstrates
that Jesus actually was aware of his unity with God and spoke as if
he were one with Him? Then it would follow that Jesus must certainly be called God become man, the God-man, in a unique sense,
insofar as he had attained the highest stage of unification within the
realm of the innermost relation between the divine and the human.
Nevertheless, the divine, while concentrated, to be sure, in the realm
of immediate consciousness, is not articulated there as it is in its
dispersion in the more peripheral fields of art, science, and so forth.
As a consequence, the so-called principal incarnation of God in Jesus
must always be completed by the revelation of the divine life in all
these other realms. Moreover, from such an identification of the
person of Jesus, nothing can be concluded about the general truth
of the gospel narrative about him. One could try, perhaps, to explain
the miracles which he worked in terms of the energy of a human
will united with the divine will. But right away the reverse comes
to mind, that is, that such a will would rather be in harmony with
God's will as it is manifested in the laws of nature and human reality.
As regards the miracles occurring to Jesus, for the most part, there
is no trace of a point of contact with the concept of his person as
the highest religious genius.

Whoever still complains that my view of the incarnation of God
as not being perfected in every respect at any time or in any individual means that the incarnation is not truly actual needs to understand better the concept of the revelation of the infinite in the
finite. The abstract basis of this concept is the category of becoming.
My critics need to see that in this category is the necessity of a
negative side, of [nonbeing]. Not even the fulfilled incarnation of 75
God in Christ assumed by the standpoint of orthodoxy lacks this
negative side; orthodoxy holds that the earthly appearance of Christ
is a transitory existence, one that does not continue.

Here I have shown how the general principles of the Hegelian philosophy do not exclude a critique of the gospel history such as I have undertaken. Now I turn to Hegel's specific statements on this subject.

# II
## HEGEL'S OPINION ON THE HISTORICAL VALUE OF THE GOSPEL HISTORY

Above all, the focal point of the gospel history, the incarnation of God in Christ, is recognized repeatedly and expressly in Hegel's writing. Hegel states, "The incarnation of the divine essence or that this (the divine essence) has essentially and immediately the shape of self-consciousness is the simple content of the absolute religion. This appears (historically) in such a way that it is the belief of the world that the spirit is there as one self-consciousness, i.e., as an actual human, that he exists for immediate certainty, that the believing consciousness sees and feels and hears this divinity. Thus, this is not imagination, but it is actual in the believer."[16]

Hegel rejects as unphilosophical, as well as unchristian, any lesser representation of Christ that does not recognize in him divinity in the full sense. He writes, "If one considers Christ to be like Socrates, then one considers him just as the Muhammadans do, as an ambassador of God, as all great heroes are ambassadors or messengers of God in a general way. When one says no more of Christ than that he was a teacher of humanity or a martyr for the truth, one does not stand at the Christian [standpoint], not at the standpoint    77
of the true religion"[17] (which, according to Hegel, is also the standpoint of the true philosophy).

God-man—"This enormous conjunction indeed totally contra-

---

[16]G. W. F. Hegel, *System der Wissenschaft: Erster Teil, die Phänomenologie des Geistes* (Bamberg and Würzburg: J. A. Goebhardt, 1807), pp. 569f. [Hereinafter cited as *Phänomenologie.*]
[17]G. W. F. Hegel, *Vorlesungen über die Philosophie der Religion*, 3 vols. in 2, vols. 11 and 12 of *Werke: Vollständige Ausgabe durch einen Verein von Freunden des Verewigten*, 18 vols. Berlin: Duncker and Humbolt, 1832-45), 2:240. [Hereinafter cited as *Philosophie der Religion.*]

dicts the understanding; the determination that God becomes human, that thereby the finite spirit has the consciousness of God in finitude itself, is the most difficult moment in religion. Indwelling in a body and dispersion into individuality appeared to be a denigration of spirit; the absolute essence which is there as one actual self-consciousness appears to have fallen from its eternal simplicity. But, actually, it has by this fact first attained its highest being; the moment of immediate existence is contained in spirit implicitly. Natural being is not an external necessity, but rather spirit, as subject in its everlasting relation to itself, has within it the determination of immediacy as the final honing of its subjectivity. For spirit is its self knowing in its alienation; its essence is the movement of maintaining equality with itself in its other-being. But this is substance insofar as it equally reflects itself in its accidents, not over against itself as opposed to something unessential, and thereby finding itself indifferently in a foreign being, but as in itself, i.e., insofar as it is subject or self."

Included in the spirituality of God, therefore, is the fact "that the finite, the human, the fragile, the other-being, the negative, is not outside of God and does not get in the way of the unity of God; rather these are other-being, negation, consciously as moments of the divine nature itself." If, according to this conception, to step out into the immediately present lies in the concept of God and spirit, this present can only be the appearance of God as human. "In sensible, worldly reality, the human alone is the spiritual reality; the human shape alone is the spiritual [shape]. Thus, if the spiritual, the divine, is to exist in a sensible shape, it must exist in the human shape. In no other way is this appearance a truthful one, not, say, as the appearance of God in a burning bush and other phenomena of this type."[18]

Thus far, Hegel seems to argue only to the unity of God with humanity in general, or to deduce that it is in the multiplicity of human individuals and personalities that God raises himself out of the night of substantiality into the day of subjectivity. This conception would be the same as Schelling's "eternal incarnation of

[18]*Phänomenologie*, pp. 569f.; *Philosophie der Religion*, 2:235ff., 253.

God," which appears to exclude, far more than to include, a particular incarnation in a single person.

Yet Hegel does reason to the particularity of Jesus as God become human. He says that the consciousness of the unity of the divine and human nature, which arose in Christianity, "had to be produced not for the standpoint of philosophical speculation, of speculative thinking, but in the form of certainty for humanity. One must have in mind this form of nonspeculative consciousness. The unity of divine and human nature had to be certain to humanity—but only what exists in internal and external perception in an immediate way is certain." Accordingly, God must appear "as a single human, in the determination of singularity, particularity. Moreover, this cannot remain with the characteristic of singularity in general, for singularity in general would again be itself universal. Singularity from this standpoint is not something universal; this exists in abstract thinking as such. But here it is a matter of the certainty of perception, of sensation, "which can grant only the singularity which appears as sensible individual."

Hegel elucidates again the same thing in the following manner: "The substantial unity of God and humanity is the implicit being of humanity; when it is this for humanity, it is beyond the immediate, everyday consciousness and knowing. Accordingly, it must stand beyond the subjective consciousness, which behaves and is defined as everyday consciousness. Precisely this explains the fact that this substantial unity must appear for others to be a single, exclusive human, not as they are all single, but as one from whom they are excluded."[19]

This line of reasoning seems to presuppose one single person, and thus this Jesus, as the God-man in a particular sense as a necessary explanation for why the Christian faith arose. "Precisely for the belief in a deep truth such as the unity of humanity with God to arise," it seems that, in Hegel's own words, "the sensible certainty of this truth must be given."[20]

This statement becomes ambiguous again because what Hegel

---

[19]*Philosophie der Religion*, 2:237f.
[20]Hoffmann, *Das Leben Jesu von Strauss*, p. 431.

had deduced and explicated throughout this argument was not so much the consciousness of the individual in whom the unity of God and humanity had become manifest, but rather the consciousness of those for whom that individual was the God-man. "This fact, that absolute spirit has given itself the shape of self-consciousness in itself and thereby also for its consciousness, appears to exist." Notice, Hegel does not say that an individual who knows his self-consciousness to be one with the divine arises, but that "it is the belief of the world that spirit as one self-consciousness, i.e., as one real human, is present. Only when the actual world-spirit has attained this knowledge of itself does this knowing also enter into its consciousness and thus enter as truth."[21] Hegel explains that, on the one hand, substance alienated itself from itself and became self-consciousness—in the development of Hellenistic religion from the incarnation of God in the plastic divine images to the destruction of the entire objective [world] of the gods in the comic consciousness of the subject. Similarly, on the other hand, the self alienated itself from itself, made itself into the nature of the thing, and thereby implicitly into a universal nature—in the unhappiness and despair, the resignation and penitence, of the world under Roman dominion.[22] It does not seem to follow that, at this point in time, an individual had to appear who knew himself as the present God, who knew his self-consciousness as that of the absolute substance. What does follow is the necessity of one who had merely the absolute propensity to see this unity of the divine and human in any of the world's marked appearances.

To be sure, this seems to contradict Hegel's judgment that the neo-Platonists had a false and fantastical mode of viewing unity with the divine. For them "self-consciousness one-sidedly grasped only its own alienation, without substance in itself similarly, on its side, alienating itself from itself and growing into consciousness." Hegel considered the neo-Platonist view inferior to the Christian standpoint at which "consciousness does not start out from its inner reality, from thought, and unite within itself the idea of God with existence,

---

[21]*Phänomenologie*, p. 568.
[22]Ibid., pp. 565f.; *Philosophie der Religion*, 2:148.

but rather it starts out from immediate existence and recognizes God in it."[23] But if one looks more closely at the actual character of the alienation of substance which Hegel said was missed in neo-Platonism and discovered in Christianity, one sees only that it is the consciousness of actual spirit, the belief of the world, that God actually became human. One sees, therefore, in Christianity a belief that the neo-Platonists did not take as a support, and, because they did not, they remained in subjective enthusiasm. Yet the assertion—that God "is there as an actual human, so that the believing consciousness sees and feels and hears this divinity"[24]—can only be taken to mean that God was believed to have existed, been seen, felt, and heard in such a way, because [for] Hegel the belief in Jesus as incarnate God begins expressly only after Jesus' death and the cessation of his sensible presence.

81

Hegel said just this in a way that increases the suspicion that he understood the divine human character less as an objective shape situated in the life of Jesus in itself than as a meaning that the hearts of his followers deposited into that life out of their subjective warrants[25] because they were disposed to find it. "The historical appearance of Christ, it will be said, can be considered simultaneously in two kinds of ways. First, as a human according to its external conditions, as he appears to nonreligious consideration, as an immediate man, in total external contingency, in total temporal relations, determinations; he was born, had the needs of all other humans as such, but he did not take up destructive tendencies, the passions and their particular inclinations. Second, according to the consideration in and with the spirit, which presses to the truth of Jesus because it has in itself this infinite split, this pain; it wants the truth, it wills to have and should have the need of truth and the certainty of truth. Thus, through belief, this individual becomes known as of a divine nature, whereby the separateness of God in the beyond is sublated. This reversal of consciousness begins with the death of Christ. The death of Christ is the focal point around which it turns; in grasping

[23]*Phänomenologie*, p. 568.
[24]Ibid.
[25]See on this Ferdinand Christian Baur, *Die christliche Gnosis: oder, Die christliche Religions-Philosophie in ihrer geschichtlichen Entwicklung* (Tübingen: Osiander, 1835).

the death lies the distinction between external comprehension and belief, which is consideration with spririt, out of the spirit of truth, the Holy Spirit. According to the former comparison, Christ is a human like Socrates, a teacher who lived a virtuous life and who brought to human consciousness that which is truthful in general and which must constitute the basis for human consciousness. But the higher consideration is [that] in Christ the divine nature was made manifest. This consciousness is reflected (as in an objective ground for proof) in such expressions as that the Son knows the Father. These expressions in themselves initially have a certain generality that exegesis can bring into the field of universal consideration. Belief, however, grasps these in their truth by the interpretation of the death of Christ. For belief is essentially the consciousness of absolute truth, of that which God is in and for himself. But God in and for himself is this life-course, the Trinity, in which the universal stands over against itself and in which it is self-identical. Belief only grasps and has the awareness that this truth existing in and for itself is perceived in the process of time in Christ (his life and death) and that this truth was first revealed through him. Through the progress of history and the forward development of world-spirit, the need to know God as spiritual reality in a universal form with his finitude stripped away has been engendered. This immediate drive, this longing, which wishes and demands something definite, is the witness of spirit and the subjective side of belief. This need and this longing demanded such a phenomenon, demanded the manifestation of God as infinite spirit in the shape of an actual human. The belief that rests on the witness of spirit, then, explicates the life of Christ. His doctrines, his words, are truly grasped and understood only by belief. And the history of Christ is narrated by those whom spirit has already filled. The miracles are grasped and narrated in this spirit, and the death of Christ is truly understood by the spirit in such a way that God in the unity of the divine and human nature was revealed in Christ."[26]

Clearly, in this passage, the objective grounds for the [interpretation] of the person and life of Christ as those of a divine human

---

[26]*Philosophie der Religion*, 2:240f., 246ff.

are plainly said to be inadequate: his life, character, and so forth, in themselves do not lead essentially beyond those of a Socrates, and his statements concerning himself allow for a different meaning. What is decisive for the intepretation of the person and life of Christ is first of all the subjective moment of the need of the will to perceive the divine life course in a single human life. This need demanded such an appearance; thus, perhaps an appearance that in itself did not have that total content was provided with it by this need itself. This is all the more probable, since the higher interpretation of the life of Jesus first occurred after his death when his followers had turned away from their objective impression of him to themselves and their own thoughts. Thus, the actual life of Jesus, in Hegel's own words, appears to be "the beginning point, the point of departure, which is to be gratefully acknowledged," but which "steps into the background" for the sake of the truth to which it leads. For, in fact, "piety can draw on everything to edify itself; the idea can issue from all reality for consciousness."[27] Consequently, this particular actuality, person, in history, from which the occasion accidentally was taken to evoke the idea in itself, has no advantage over other histories and no relation to the idea that is essentially closer than others.

Hegel defined more exactly the transition that occurred with the death of Christ as follows: In his friends and acquaintances, whom he instructed, Jesus awoke "the presentiment, the representation, the wish for a new kingdom, a new heaven and a new earth, a new world," of the kingdom of God. "The basic determination in this kingdom of God is the presence of God so that the members of this kingdom experience not only love for humans, but also the awareness that God is love. Therein it is even said that God is present, that this presence [must] exist as one's own feeling, as self-feeling. Because, on the one side, this presence is a need and a feeling, on the other side, the subject must also distinguish itself from it; the subject must distinguish from itself this presence of God, but in such a way that this presence is certain, and this certainty can be present under these conditions only in the mode of sensible ap-

84

---

[27]Ibid., pp. 262, 265.

pearance."[28] As a single human who was sensibly living, the human side of his presence dominated, and the God-man in him could not yet be recognized. With his death, this hindrance fell away, on the one side. Yet, on the other side, the task of finding the meaning of his death presented itself to the consciousness of his followers.

Because of the perspective the living Jesus had already given his followers, the meaning of his death could not be for them a merely moral relation, such as martyrdom for the truth or repression by injustice. It had to be a religious relation, which is that of the infinite relation to God as he is present in his kingdom. Thus the death of Christ was given "this meaning—that Christ was the God-man, that Christ was the God who at the same time possessed a human nature, indeed even unto death. Humanity becomes conscious in this history that the human is the immediate, present God, and specifically, in such a way, that in this history, as spirit grasps it, even the presentation of the process is a presentation of that which humanity is, which spirit is. To be implicitly God and dead—this mediation, by which the human is stripped away, and the other side returns what exists in itself to itself, and so for the first time spirit exists."[29]

The fact that the unity of the divine and the human is perceived in the one person of Jesus is for Hegel not only an act of faith, but also clearly a lower standpoint from which there must be an ascent to a higher one. "That absolute spirit in its existence as one single individual, or rather as a particular individual, represents the [nature] of spirit, belongs," according to Hegel, "to the element of representation."[30] The spirit that knows itself as spirit, the God become man, is in its first immediate appearance "this single self-consciousness, opposed to the universal. It is the one which excludes all others. For the consciousness for which it is present, it has the still unresolved form of a sensible other. This other does not yet know spirit as its own; since it is single self, spirit is not yet present as equally universal, as the self of everyone. In other words, the shape does

---

[28]Ibid., pp. 247f.
[29]Ibid., pp. 249, 253.
[30]*Phänomenologie*, p. 568.

not yet have the form of the concept, i.e., of the universal self, of the self that in its immediate actuality is at the same time sublated. It does not have the form of thinking, of universality, without the self being lost in these."[31]

Reconciliation is implicitly contained in the "universal idea of God" as the being which is identical with itself in its other-being, or in that "knowledge of nature as the untrue existence of spirit. But for the nonconceiving self-consciousness, that which is implicit in this idea is the form of an existing being and one represented by it." In order to become certain for the everyday consciousness, "the idea of God must be represented as something historical, as one, which in its appearance, has been fulfilled on earth. For this everyday consciousness, conceiving is not an apprehending of this concept, which knows the sublated natural being as universal and therefore as reconciled with itself. On the contrary, it is an apprehending of that representation that the divine essence is reconciled with its existence through the event of the self-alienation of the divine essence, through its actual incarnation and death."[32] This first, immediate form, in which consciousness exists in the presence of spirit, must now, however, be sublated. The particular must become the universal. But "the closest and immediate form" of this sublation into universality "is not yet the form of thinking itself, of the concept as concept"; [rather] it is the raising of existence out of the sensuous individual presence into the representation of all individuals. In other words, the God-man, first present as a sensible "this," now lives in the consciousness of all members of his community. But this raising through "the past, distancing," and memory is "only an imperfect form in which the immediate mode is mediated or is posited as universal. This mode is only superficially submerged into the element of thinking. It is preserved in the element of thinking as a sensuous mode (the individual, although existing in the universal consciousness of the community, is still maintained as a single individual), and is not yet unified with the nature of thinking."[33]

86

---

[31]Ibid., p. 572.
[32]Ibid., pp. 588ff; *Philosophie der Religion*, 2:259.
[33]*Phänomenologie*, pp. 572f.

The further stage, and the true one, arrives first when everyone allows that which they represented as having happened in the single life to be represented and happen in themselves. This stage arrives when they "transfigure the death (of Jesus) from that which it immediately signified, i.e., the nonbeing of this single person, into the universality of the spirit that lives in their community and daily dies and is resurrected in it." But then, because this process is transposed into the element of self-consciousness, this spirit "does not actually die, as the particular is represented to have actually died, but its particularity perishes in its universality, that is, in its knowing, which is the essence that reconciles itself with itself."[34] Secondly, at this stage, that which the believing consciousness represented as having been present in another and as having been imparted to the others for their own sake, conceiving thinking comes to recognize as lying implicitly in the essence and concept of humanity and as something that comes to actuality in that one person in the past as in all individual humans only out of this ground.

Thus, this stage of representation is probably the topic of the following expression of Hegel: "In the pantheism of India, there occur innumerable incarnations because subjectivity, the human being, is taken only as an accidental form of God. But God as spirit contains [in] himself the moment of subjectivity, of individuality. Therefore, also, his appearance can only be an individual one; it can only occur once."[35] It is impossible to conclude from this statement that the incarnation of God in a particular individual should be considered more truthful than an incarnation in the totality of humans. On the contrary, the falseness of the (divine-human) individuality, which has vanished, was contrasted very explicitly with the truth of the universal singleness.[36] This Hegelian proposition on pantheism, therefore, can mean to say only this much: To the representing consciousness the implicit appears as that which is separated in the beyond, and therefore its implicit divinity appears to

87

---

[34] Ibid., p. 589.

[35] *Philosophie der Religion*, 2:236f.

[36] *Phänomenologie*, p. 165. See. G. W. F. Hegel, *Vorlesungen über die Geschichte der Philosophie*, ed. D. Karl Ludwig Michelet, 3 vols. (Berlin: Duncker and Humbolt, 1833-36), 3:209. [Hereinafter cited as *Geschichte der Philosophie*.]

be an incarnation of God standing outside of it. Thus it can represent this incarnate God either as one, or as several, individuals (but not as all individuals, because by this conception the alienation between the divine and the human would be overcome). Since singleness lies nearer than indefinite multiplicity to the concept, which demands universality, the belief that one human represents the divine human unity lies closer to the proposition that humanity is the revealed God than does the other conviction, which says that several humans represent this unity.

In this respect, a distinction made by Hegel in various forms is of special importance. He says that the content of Christian belief has two parts, which must be kept distinct. "The one part is what the Church teaches as dogma, that is, the doctrine about the nature of God, that God is triune; to this doctrine belongs the appearance of God in the world and in the flesh as well as the relation of humanity to this divine nature, to its blessedness and divinity. This part of Christian belief contains eternal truths and is of absolute interest for humanity. The content of this part is essentially speculative, and it can be an object only for the speculative concept. The other part, in which belief is also demanded, is related to external representation; to this part belongs the entire range of the historical, the history in the Old and New Testaments and the history of the Church, and so on. Belief in all this finitude is probably [required]. Thus, a person would be considered a free thinker or an atheist if he did not believe that in paradise Adam ate the apple.[37] Both parts of belief are placed on one level. The fact that belief in both parts is required causes the decay of the Church and of faith. When such external representations are retained, it cannot fail that contradictions become evident."[38]

Hegel makes use of the same distinction when, in another place, he states, "The question of the truth of the Christian religion immediately divides into two parts: (1) Is it true in general that God

88

---

[37] In another place (*Philosophie der Religion*, 2:217), Hegel comments: "It is represented that the first human did this. Again this is to speak in this sensible manner; according to thought the first human is called the human as human, not any single or contingent one out of many, but the absolutely first, the human according to its concept."

[38] *Geschichte der Philosophie*, 3:249.

does not exist without the Son, and that God has sent him into the
world? and (2) Was this Jesus of Nazareth, the carpenter's son, the
Son of God, the Christ? Most of the time these two questions are
so confused that if Jesus were not the Son sent by God, and if this
were impossible to prove of him, there would be no truth to God's
sending of his Son. Either we would have to await another Son, if
indeed one is to come to exist, if there is a promise, i.e., if it is
necessary in and for itself in the concept or in the idea. Or, rather,
since the accuracy of the idea is made dependent on the proof of
this sending, [if this cannot be proven] there is really nothing more
to think about with regard to it. But, before dismissing the idea of
God sending his Son into the world, we must ask whether such an
appearance is true in and for itself. It is true, because God as Spirit
is triune. He is this manifesting, this self-objectifying, this remaining
self-identical in this objectifying; he is eternal love."[39]

89          [The answer] to the question about the implicit truth of God's
sending his Son, or the "verification of this side" of Christian belief,
is from the standpoint of the believing consciousness "only an inner
verification, the witness of spirit." Philosophy immediately has to
"explicate" and to raise this to the "element of thinking." The other
side, the historical, does not have the spirit or philosophy for its
verification. For this it has "the historical, juridical way of attesting
to a fact, that is, sense certainty"—the moral uprightness of the
eyewitnesses, the authenticity of the tradition, and so forth. But
"the verification of the sensible, whatever content it may have, remains subject to an infinite series of objections, because at the basis
of this sensible external lies what is contrary to spirit and to consciousness. Here consciousness and object are separate, and this
fundamental split carries with it the possibility of error, deception,
and the lack of education necessary to grasp the fact correctly. Thus,
doubts will always be present. Sensible content is not certain in itself
because it does not exist through spirit; that is, it has another ground
and is not posited through the concept. It is thought that one must
get to the proof by a comparison of all the witnesses and circumstances, or that bases for deciding for one or the other must be

---

[39]*Philosophie der Religion*, 2:260f.

found." But the historical witnesses which we have discussed here cannot "ever give us the degree of certainty that newspaper accounts give us on any one event." It is totally wrong to think "that verification is a matter of the materiality of phenomena and of the historical and to think that the verification of spirit and its truth lie in such narratives which are represented as historical according to the historical method. The truth of spirit stands on its own, even though it has a historical point of departure. What spirit is to believe must not be sensible belief; sensible phenomena are subordinate to what is true for spirit. As spirit begins from the sensible, and comes to evaluate it, its relation to the [sensible] is at the same time a negative relation (i.e., it lowers it to an indifferent reality which is not the truth and 'is not posited through the concept'—it either can or cannot have happened, and historical critique has to decide this). This is its principal determination."[40]

90

After such clear statements, what can Hegel be saying to the contrary when he writes: "There also exists a type of the historical that is a divine history, and it exists in such a way that it should be a history in the true sense (in distinction from the Greek myths). The history of Christ is valued not merely as a myth, according to the mode of images, but as something totally historical"?[41] Here the expressions "should be" and "is valued" lead to ambiguity, and it is impossible to know from what follows whether Hegel is not just speaking about the way in which representation conceives this history. Moreover, he never says that the narratives of the life of Jesus in all their parts are to be taken as historical, nor does he draw a line up to which they should be. In any case, if Hegel had accepted for himself everything in these narratives without distinction as historical, then, according to what has been said previously, he would not have done so on the authority of the concept or of the conclusions of his system. Rather, he would have had to have done so on the authority of historical research, and, therefore, in order to have been consistent, he would have had to leave us free to reach different conclusions.

---

[40]Ibid., 2:2ɔ9, 260ff.; *Phänomenologie*, pp. 418f.
[41]Ibid., 1:82. This passage is cited against me by Karl Wilhelm Ernst in his *Brief an eine Dame über die Hegelische Philosophie* (Berlin: Morin, 1837), p. 72 note.

But it is not true that Hegel even once accepted the entire history of Jesus as it was reported in the Gospels. If we look back we see that he wrote about the supernatural conception of Jesus: "If one [will] make use of relations taken from natural conception, it can be said of this spirit, which has abandoned the form of substance and stepped into existence in the shape of self-consciousness, that he has an actual mother but a father existing implicitly. For actuality, or self-consciousness, and the implicit as substance are spirit's two moments, and through their natural alienation, each becoming the other, Christ entered existence as this, their unity."[42] Surely, the miraculous fact of his conception is not deduced in this statement; rather, the narrative of his conception is allegorized.

On the miracles that fill up the middle of *The Life of Jesus* we read the following in Hegel: "Sensible verification contributes nothing to the fact that it is an essential determination of the nature of God himself (to become human). The miracles belong to this sensible verification since they are of importance for the empirical, external consciousness of belief. This is a different field, a different ground, from that of spirit. Because humans commonly imagine God as a power of nature, they also imagine that this individual had to witness to himself by the shining phenomena of miracles, i.e., by his absolute power over nature. Christ says, 'You want to see miracles.' It is not a matter of signs and miracles. He rejects them. Moreover, according to their nature, miracles are an external, spiritless mode of witness. It is correct to say that God and his power are present in nature in and according to eternal laws, and that the real miracle is spirit itself. Surely, animal nature is a miracle in comparison with vegetable nature, and, even more, spirit is a miracle in comparison with life as merely sentient nature."[43] When one takes into account Hegel's remark about the difficulty, and indeed the impossibility of historical proof (which he made in another place[44] and which we quoted above), it is clear that he does not merely deny miracles' power to establish dogma, but he also brings into doubt their historical reality.

---

[42]*Phänomenologie*, p. 567.
[43]*Philosophie der Religion*, 2:256.
[44]Ibid., p. 264.

Just as immaterial as miracles for the truth of Christian belief, [according] to Hegel, are the facts of the resurrection and the ascension of Jesus. He states, "If one considers the resurrection and ascension of Christ to be sensible events, then, in respect to sensible reality, it is a matter not of the relation of historical verification to these phenomena (whether they can be established as external, historical facts), but rather of the relation between both sensible verification and sensible events together to spirit, to spiritual content."[45] That is to say, what is at issue is whether or not the dogmatic truth of the ideas, which is seen in and constitutes the content of the resurrection and ascension, is dependent on the historical verifiability or lack of verifiability of these events. Surely, the conception of the resurrection and ascension of Jesus as external, sensible facts is not the true conception. "The resurrection belongs essentially to belief; after his resurrection, Christ appeared only to his friends. This is not external history for unbelief; only for belief is this an appearance."[46]

Clearly, Hegel did not understand the representations of the resurrection and ascension of Jesus as providing a reversal in the consciousness of his disciples, but rather as proceeding out of this reversal. After the death of Jesus "spirit" informed the disciples that they had perceived in the life course of Jesus the nature of spirit. "This death"—in Hegel's expression—"seen in this way is the death that is the transition to glory, to glorification, which is however only the reestablishment of the original glory. Death, the negative, is the mediating element by which the original exaltation is assumed to be attained. Thereby, the history of the resurrection and the ascension of Christ to the right hand of God begins at the point where this history attains a spiritual interpretation."[47]

The resurrection of Jesus is for Hegel at all times only the fact that the God-man "has arisen in spirit, just as previously he arose as sensibly existing for consciousness," that is, he has become the "universal self-consciousness of the community." The [ascension]

---

[45]Ibid.
[46]Ibid., p. 250.
[47]Ibid., pp. 252f.

and raising to the right hand of God means only that "the abstract (divine) essence," which by its appearance as human "was alienated from itself and had natural existence in the actuality of the self, now sublates its other-being (the sensible presence) by the second reversal (death)." The ascension means that the God who has stepped outside of himself returns into himself, or, much better, that he shows that this stepping outside of himself does not destroy his unity with himself, because it is at the same time eternally a returning back into himself.[48]

Notwithstanding Hegel's indifference and skeptical relation to the most important pieces of the gospel history, he does not just hold firmly to the incarnation of God in general, but also to the appearance of God in the flesh, the God "come forward in this human (Jesus), in this place, at this time."[49] Therefore, his propositions cited above—that the spirit knowing itself as spirit or, what is the same thing, the human knowing himself as God, is in its first, immediate appearance "a single self-consciousness opposing the universal, and one excluding all others"—are not to be understood to say merely that humans represent this appearance in this way. These propositions must be understood to say also that the consciousness of spirit knowing itself as spirit actually first appeared as a consequence of a single being, through which it immediately imparted itself to the other. And yet this apparently definite explanation is once again made ambiguous, or at least it must be extremely qualified, by passages like the following: "What the self-revealing spirit is in and for itself is not brought forward because his rich life is, so to speak, unravelled in the Christian community and followed back to its first threads, perhaps to representations of the first imperfect community, or all the way back to what the actual man spoke. The instinct to attain the concept is at the basis of this desire to reach the first threads, but it confuses the origin of the concept as the immediate existence of its first appearance with the simplicity of the concept. The concept is not reached through this impoverishing [of the] life of the spirit, through this removal of the representation of

94

---

[48]*Phänomenologie*, pp. 573, 583f., 389.
[49]*Philosophie der Religion*, 2:240.

the community and its actions with regard to it. What arises instead of the concept is the bare externality and singleness, the historical mode of immediate appearance, and the spiritless recollection of a single, most common shape and its past. One can almost say that when one traces Christianity back to this first appearance, it is brought to the standpoint of a lack of spirituality."[50] This is exactly the position of Schelling, which we previously cited, that the first realization of the Christian principle in the New Testament writings is incomplete.

If we summarize the view of Hegel on the gospel history and the historical person of Jesus in the light of these conflicting quotes, the following conclusions can be drawn:

1. A definite need arising at a certain time in the course of world history to perceive the unity of the divine and the human in sensible presence contributed most of all to the development of the perception that recognizes in the man Jesus the present God and in his life the explication of the divine life.

2. The individual narrated events of the life of Jesus are to be distinguished from their absolute significance; this significance is independent of their historical reality or unreality. Thus, the research in these matters is to be left completely to critique, which, however, can never attain a completely firm conclusion because of the nature of the subject.

3. Yet the person of Jesus still retains the significance that the unity of the divine and the human has appeared in him as in no other person. It is only that Hegel left in what way and to what extent Jesus retains this significance partly undefined, and partly limited by the fact that he explained the content of the consciousness of Christ as incomplete when compared with the consciousness that immediately began its gradual development in the Christian community.

---

[50]*Phänomenologie*, p. 574f.; *Geschichte der Philosophie*, 3:111.

# III
## DIFFERENT CHRISTOLOGICAL DIRECTIONS
## WITHIN THE HEGELIAN SCHOOL

Given what we saw in the previous section—Hegel's undeniable lack of clarity about the person and history of Jesus, and the identity of his principle and system with Schelling's, which exists along with the distinctions between them—it is not surprising that the Hegelian school has gone in different directions on Christology. To the question of whether and to what extent the gospel history is proven as history by the idea of the unity of the divine and human natures, there are three possible answers: either the entirety of the history is proven by this concept, or merely a part of it, or finally, that neither as a whole nor in part is it to be confirmed as historical by the idea. If each of these answers and directions were indeed represented by a branch of the Hegelian school, then, using the traditional analogy, the first direction, as standing closest to the long-established system, could be named the right, the third direction named the left, and the second named the center.

### 1. The Right Side of the Hegelian School
### and Its Relation to Critique

The far right side of the Hegelian school, especially in theology, is championed preeminently by Professor Göschel. In his famous *Aphorisms*, he already had made [the attempt] to reconcile religious belief with philosophical knowing by bringing the austerity of the concept closer to the geniality of the representation.[51] He showed the believer how the most genuine and beloved pieces of dogma,

---

[51][Carl Göschel, *Aphorismen über Nichtwissen und absolutes Wissen im Verhältnis zur christlichen Glaubenserkenntnis* (Berlin: Franklin, 1829).]

which the believer thought to be threatened by speculation, are instead recognized in their full worth by it. Hegel, delighted over this first salutation presented by religion to his philosophy, which he was rightly aware that he deserved, gave a friendly response in his famous review of Göschel's book.[52] But Hegel must have been immediately aware that in the book, which he praised, the distinction between concept and representation, belief and knowlege, had been placed too much in the background in favor of their identity. Since the appearance of the review, Göschel, as the one recognized and esteemed highly by Hegel, has risen to become one of the principal spokesmen of the school, and he has continued to work in the adopted direction to see that a share of "the seat and vote in the absolute concept goes to the representation."[53]

Therefore, Göschel is especially concerned to get full recognition for the historical element in Christianity, for the biblical, and, in particular for the new Testament history in the face of the recent critique. He knows how to attribute doubts about this history to a deep perversity, which he describes in the following terms: "The relation of the spirit to eternity (in that this relation is essential to the nature of spirit) itself becomes once again for the doubter a temptation and a fall, an act of pride, when he mistakes the meaning of time as it is now for this relation and when he denies as historical fact the deeds of God in this finite time."[54] This argument can certainly seem to make the battle against critique easier, because everyone [knows] that that which denies the appearance of the infinite in the finite and of divine deeds in time is false. But, in fact, nothing is gained by this charge of perversity, because this standpoint is by no means that of critique.

97

Critique does not at all struggle against the acknowledgment of divine deeds in history. On the contrary, because from its standpoint all history is considered to be divine activity and the emergence of

---

[52][Hegel's review of Göschel's *Aphorismen* can be found in his *Berliner Schriften, 1818-1831*, vol. 2 of *Sämtliche Werke*, new critical edition by Johannes Hoffmeister (Hamburg: Felix Meiner, 1956).]

[53]See "Erstes und Letztes. Ein Glaubensbekenntniss der speculativen Philosophie, von C. F. Göschel," in Bruno Bauer's *Zeitschrift für Speculative Theologie*, vol. 1, bk. 1, p. 92.

[54]Ibid., p. 90.

the eternal into time, critique is not willing to grant to any single
history *kat' exokan* this predicate. Certainly, it distinguishes stages
and modes of the manifestation of God in history—in one time a
certain aspect of the divine life comes forward, while in another time
a different aspect appears, and its spiritual content penetrates here
more energetically than there. It is only that critique cannot accept
the theory that any one part of history is distinguished as an immediate divine revelation from all the other parts as merely mediate
revelations or as sacred history from profane history. Looking at the
whole broad plain of events and at the strokes of the divine on the
entire vast painting, critique cannot persuade itself that it is correct
to cut a piece out of this canvas anywhere and encircle it with a tiny
gold frame. It attributes any attempt to do this to narrowness of
vision.

Göschel goes on to say that "whoever falls into this trap of
misunderstanding the relation of spirit to eternity is probably used
to saying that these finite deeds are incompatible with the infinity
of God instead of perceiving in them precisely the factual self-low-
ering of God." This assertion is refuted by what I just said. As he
states it, this criticism is completely wrong. In no way do we consider
God's appearance in the finite to be incompatible with his infinity;
it is only that we cannot accept the idea that the infinite reaches full
presentation in any one single finite being. We have a concept of
the relation of the infinite and the finite whereby that which is present
in the infinite and in the divine idea, ideally and collected into one,
exists in finite reality and in the real world, dispersed into multiplicity. Therefore, whoever wants to discover the content of the
infinite in the finite should not reach after one single phenomenon
98      exclusively, [but] he must collect the infinite content out of its
totality.[55]

Again, this is not to deny that there are certain nodal points in

---

[55]See Karl Rosenkranz, *Enzyklopädie der theologischen Wissenschaft* (Halle: C. A.
Schwetschke, 1831), p. 37: "An essence is outside of time but its appearance is revealed
in time. Similarly that which appears is not a momentary reality, passing away once;
rather as a manifestation of the essence by which it is posited it is permanent reality.
One must not think that the single phenomenon, each for itself as single, reveals
essence. Only the totality of phenomena in which the contingency and deficiency of
single existents are canceled reveals this."

the realm of finite being in which a number of the otherwise dispersed threads of the divine life run together. For example, such nodal points exist within the nature of humanity in the history of particular peoples and epochs, within all peoples and epochs in the history of religion as it relates to the rest of history, and, once more, within the history of religion itself in the history of the origin of Christianity. But this type of relationship is totally different from the one our critics want us to find between the gospel history and the rest of history. Göschel describes the type of relationship they seek as follows: "These finite facts are fully and precisely fitting to the fallen finite spirit, and, thereby, to God's lowering himself into finite spirit. Therefore, it is the greatest perversity of all that while God lowers himself to the finite, the human raises himself above it because he wants to raise God above it. This perverted elevation belongs to the aftereffects of the fall, namely, the tendency to want to be eternal immediately instead of being subordinate to the succession of developments to which the Son of God himself has lowered himself."[56]—This whole discussion of God and the finite, as edifying as it is, does not impress us because it does not have anything to do with us.

Göschel also remarks: "At the [root] of the sensible phenomenon or the representation, there does not lie a universal truth, but rather the truth of spirit which is individuality. This truth of spirit is not a subjective idea, which proceeds from individual subjects. On the contrary, the idea is objective for these subjects because it proceeds from the absolute subject. Thus, even the sensible appearance of this truth is this truth itself in its fullness, and in a manner fully fitting to its purpose and concept." This remark of Göschel's seems to be in agreement with that made by another member of the right wing of the Hegelian school, Gabler. He wrote in Latin:

> Strauss, however, appears to me to have understood least that which Hegel intended and to have erred most about that which he wanted to value, i.e., about those things which pertain to the idea, to the entire process of human

99

---

[56]Ibid., pp. 90f.

cognition alone. Strauss referred to human thought, which sees the necessity of the divine reality as though God, who created the nature of existing phenomena as well as those things which pertain to the manifestation and revelation of the very divine mind as mind, were powerless to effect the existence of that mind in phenomena. That is, he considers this very divine mind itself incapable of being totally and integrally expressed and developed in a particular human born into its light and living in it, and, in turn, sublated by it. Or, if Strauss does not envisage this sort of impotent creator God, then he clearly does deny that the perfection of human nature allows it to receive into itself, fully and truly, that which belongs only to human thought, i.e., that very divine mind.[57]

This criticism means that I comprehend the idea, namely, the idea of the unity of the divine and human nature, as a merely subjective idea. According to Göschel and Gabler, because I do not recognize the idea as completely realized in one single human, but only in the totality of humanity, my conception of the idea is subjective since this totality of humanity is never given actually, but always exists only in thought.[58]

Let us consider a moment, what if the idea that attained complete presentation in one individual is the only one that could be considered to be realized? Then, presupposing the complete realization of [the idea] of divine humanity in the person of Jesus, this would be the only idea that would enjoy reality, because all other ideas (whatever names they might have) would have to submit to having their reality collected from a number of phenomena. Indeed, the idea of divine humanity itself, even if Christ were the God-man in the full sense, would still have to be denied reality if there is supposed to be no reality present wherever thinking has to integrate a series of single phenomena in order to find it. For even in Christ's life, the divine humanity could not be actual in the total fullness of its content at every moment. In order to see its total reality in him,

100

---

[57]Gabler, *De Verae*, p. 42 note.
[58]See Hoffmann, *Das Leben Jesu von Strauss*, p. 435.

we must reflectively integrate the various moments of his life. Thus, even here, if the right-wing canon is respected, the reality of the idea would be, in the final instance, only a reality in thought. If, however, one affirms that the idea was realized in Christ as presupposed [that is, objectively, not only in thought], in spite of the fact that it was not realized completely at any single moment, then one must admit that the idea can exist in this way in humanity, even if it does not come to presentation in any single point of time, space, or individual.

What does it mean, then, when Göschel and Gabler refuse to recognize that the idea of the unity of the divine and human is truly realized in humanity because they object to the fact of its dispersion in a multiplicity of individuals? Clearly, they are guilty of what they so readily charge me; they, much more than I, have fallen back to Kant's standpoint. Kant declared the idea to be a mere "ought" precisely because he was incapable of synthetically comprehending its presentation in a mass of separated phenomena which mutually complete each other and form the unity of a true actuality. One can also identify this perspective as a nominalistic dependence on empirical individualities. Moreover, one can say that, from the perspective of true realism, the truly real is not this or that human but the universal humanity, and, consequently, the realization of the idea in this universal humanity is the true realization.

Placing himself on the same side of the Hegelian school with Göschel and Gabler is Licentiate Bauer, the reviewer of my *Life of Jesus* in the *Jahrbücher für wissenschaftliche Kritik* [*Yearbooks for Scientific Critique*].[59] To be sure, he concedes to my critique, as he puts it, its full "human right" as a necessary judgment on the previous shapes of the theological consciousness, and he complains that for the most part my opponents, whom he has reviewed (especially those working from the premises of supernaturalism), do not recognize this right. Bauer goes on to describe in a relevant and gratifying way how none of the different theological tendencies ought to absolve themselves of the guilt of this latest critique (if it truly is to be a guilt) and how

101

---

[59]See Bruno Bauer's review of my *Life of Jesus* in *JWK* (December 1835), nos. 109-13; (May 1836), nos. 86-88; and (March 1837), nos. 41-43.

all of them, from their different sides, have worked to a conclusion like it. The critique of the gospel history would have a divine right as well as a human one, according to Bauer, if it were based on the firm purpose—or rather, if it sustained this purpose, which certainly could be its original presupposition—to comprehend the sacred history and to recognize it in its necessity and rationality as a development of the proper nature of spirit. He continues: "It takes only a brief look to see that this purpose is lost in the process by which critique tries to mediate the object of belief and the historical content of scripture with self-consciousness. Insofar as it wants to be knowledge, critique immediately in its initial procedure falls away from this purpose, denies itself, and surrenders its divine right. Critique wants to attain insight as the insuperable and all-surmounting power of self-consciousness over the objective; it wants to allow nothing to stand over against it as an impenetrable object. On the contrary, it tries to negate the hardened objectivity in the object and to recognize itself in it. But as it supervenes in that way upon the object, critique becomes snagged in the object's impenetrability or in its difficulty, and, for that reason it, therefore, claims that the object is unreal and impossible. But openly to pronounce the object to be impossible because of its difficulty [seems] too much like a flight away from reality for critique to be satisfied in doing so."[60]

102

So critique is supposed to approach its task with the firm purpose of finding the object that it is about to examine absolutely testworthy. A critique that in the course of its operation falls away from this purpose, hits a snag in its object, and separates a part of it out as being not sound, would be, just because of that, a false critique. This argument seems to me to represent the special case of theological critique. In other realms of critique, this law is never enforced. A person studying peas or lentils, for example, can hardly be blamed for separating out a part of them—as long as this part contains really damaged or foreign kernels. No one has ever demanded that such a researcher had to find all the kernels that he had in hand to be good. If that were the case, then it would be better to omit entirely the classifying process. By all means, critique would

---

[60]Bauer, *JWK* (December 1835), no. 111, pp. 891f.

be just as perverse if it did what Bauer accuses mine of doing. He claims that "from the beginning or *a priori*" my critique posits the object as something other than it is, remains standing by itself to one side, and, without going into the object, "only criticizes it but never once undertakes the attempt to know it." Putting off for the moment the question of whether or not this accusation really bears on my critique, I want to point out that presupposing the untenability of the object of critique is not a hair closer to the truth than the contrary position, which Bauer advocates, i.e., presupposing that this object is one from which nothing is to be rejected. If there is to be a critique at all, it ought not to adopt either one of these presuppositions. It should let the question of whether it [finds] its object completely trustworthy, or completely falsified, or partly one, partly the other, be determined by the process and result of research. Or, if critique is not to be entirely without presupposition, then its sole presupposition can be that it is always possible to find something in its object that does not withstand its examination. I would like to know how one could define critique at all, how one could give a general description of it, without at the same time assuming the presupposition of its possibility, or accepting its right to some degree to hit a snag in its object.

    As Bauer says, I attribute the blame for my negative relation to the object of my critique, not to myself, but "to the content (of the gospel history) in its inappropriateness to the demands and determinations of self-consciousness, which makes itself evident from the beginning."[61] Thus, to find the reason why the biblical critic should bring to his task, and sustain through it, the purpose of a solely positive relation to an object, Bauer must look in the specific nature of the object of research, because it can by no means lie in the general nature of critique. In this case, the absolute character of Christianity, therefore, must from the outset exclude the possibility of finite, particularly unhistorical, sections in the reports of its origin; with this presupposition, which is made in no other realm of research, critique must approach at least the Bible. When put more precisely this is to say that critique is not at all applicable to the

103

---

[61]Ibid., p. 900.

gospel history or to any biblical history. There cannot even be a biblical critique; for a critique that presupposes its object to be absolute and without fault is precisely no critique.[62]

104      [For all that,] the reviewer thinks that I was not even inclined to proceed with what he considers to be the proper presupposition in my critical work. If only I had seriously made the attempt in the course of my work to enter into the gospel history and understand it as rational, the result of my research would have been totally different. Since, on the contrary, I took up a solely judgmental position toward the gospel content, and in no way made the attempt to comprehend it, it is no wonder that I could not convince myself of its historical character. I am very grateful to Bauer for giving me an example of how I ought to have treated the gospel history in order to comprehend it as rational and actual in his introduction to the narrative of the supernatural conception of Jesus.[63]

Bauer begins with Schleiermacher's critique of this narrative, which I used in *The Life of Jesus*, and he attempts to find in it points of view that only need to be carried through to their true meaning in order to be shifted from a critique of dogma into its defense. For example, although Schleiermacher proclaimed, as would Bauer, that the physiological law of procreation is absolute, he probably was very well aware also that "every beginning of a human life can be explained in two different ways—as an event within the small circle of parentage and society, to which it immediately belongs, and as a fact of human nature in general." Thereupon, Professor Bauer concedes, of course, that "these two ways are in fact and appearance only one in that the beginning of an individual life within the circle of the family, a race, a tribe, or a people is at the same time no less a fact of human nature in general, because this nature realizes itself in individuals." Bauer thinks it is not enough to comprehend the procreation of Christ as a fact of universal human nature only in the

---

[62]See Bruno Bauer's opposition to the distinction of the so-called true critique from skeptical critique in his remarks on the review of Pastor Lange's book, *Über den geschichtlichen Character der kanonischen Evangelien, insbesondere der Kindheitgeschichte Jesu; mit besonderer Beziehung auf das Leben Jesu von D.F. Strauss*, which appeared in *Evangelische Kirchenzeitung* (July 1836), nos. 55-58, pp. 52f. note.
[63]Bauer, *JWK* (December 1836), no. 111, pp. 892ff.

sense that it would have been mediated by the sexual activity of a single pair of humans. The adequate and exhaustive expression of human nature in general, or of its universal concept, never appears "in the product [of these] two factors." This product is limited by the natural place of birth from which it has issued, and, through this limitation which is posited together with nature, it is immediately placed into the general relationship of universal sinfulness.

One can see right away what Bauer's problem is here: an act of human procreation mediated by individuals does not give us Christ as the Church represents him. Consequently, a conception without this mediation must have taken place. This way of arguing is just like that of the natural scientist who expressed the opinion that humanity would have to succeed once more in sailing to the moon and stars. When asked to explain the basis for such an audacious hope, the scientist answered: Because in no other way could humans procure knowledge about these cosmic bodies. Besides, it would also follow from Bauer's premises that Christ must have been engendered not only without a father, but also without a mother, he must have proceeded merely out of the universal human nature as such, that is, to be precise, he must have fallen from heaven, just as many Gnostics assume.

But all this puts off the issue. Let us return to the place where we left Bauer's argument. It is not only the attainment of the perfection of the product that he believes to be compromised by the accepting of a natural conception of Jesus. He also holds that "the assumption that the conception of Christ was mediated by the sexual activity of a single family circle means that the beginning of his life is as arbitrary and contingent as any individual beginning of life. Given this assumption, one could probably still speak of a type of necessity which determined the coming forth of Christ. But this type of necessity always remains merely externally conditioned and extrinsic to the birth unless the birth is in itself the perfect expression of this necessity itself."

This example shows once more that, while these right-wing Hegelians think that [they] are on the highest pinnacle of speculation, they unconsciously slip down to the everyday plain of common

105

106

representation. Just as they argue that no true realization of the idea
is found where it is not fully present in one individual and cannot
be sorted out from the rest of humanity, so here they argue that
there is no necessity if it does not exist for itself, separated from all
contingencies. But just as we argued that speculative thinking is
distinguished from popular representation because it can hold together, in the full actuality of the idea, the multitude of existences,
which are incomplete in themselves, we argue here that speculation
recognizes inner necessity in precisely the freest play of contingency.

It is the worst kind of concept of necessity, or better put, the
worst representation of it, that has to exclude contingency, instead
of assuming it into necessity as a moment. All great events of world
history have in them this aspect of contingency: this height of the
sun, this velocity of the wind, this decision of a popular battle, the
flight of an arrow or a bullet, the fall of a stone, ends a world-
historical life. Yet we did not give up the assumption of a higher
necessity even to these events. Would we lose a world-historical
necessity of the birth of Jesus if we have him engendered by human
parents? We can imagine that his parents, and even his grandparents,
might not have met one another and then Jesus as their progeny
would not have been born. But, in order to exclude all contingencies
from his birth, do we have to have such fantasies as those about
God himself depositing Jesus in the world, single-handedly, as it
were? In this case, God, also acting single-handedly, would have
had to have carried Jesus throughout his entire life. If God had not
done so, there would have been the chance that Jesus, just as any
other human, could have had an accident before growing up.

107        "[When] the birth (of Jesus) is considered as the result of a
limited realm," continues Professor Bauer, "its necessity cannot be
presented, and thus one is inevitably forced into agreement with the
claims of critique; what critique leaves unsaid is what can be derived
from reflection on the birth of Jesus as a fact of human nature in
general." Of course, critique leaves this unsaid because it cannot
derive anything meaningful from this—at least as it is undertaken
by the right-wing Hegelians. Critique does not hope to get "apple"
from the species appletree as such but always only from a single

appletree. Similarly, it cannot fathom how "human nature in general" might produce an individual without the agency of individuals.

But, according to Bauer, this act of production involved in the birth of Jesus is not to be attributed to universal human nature as such. On the contrary, the power of producing the God-man is expressly denied to universal human nature in the two principal forms that it took during Jesus' time, i.e., paganism and Judaism. In the pagan Roman world "the natural determinations of human nature were effaced and raised to a uniform universality. The narrow spirit of race, tribe, and people had given up the limits immediately determined by nature and had immersed themselves in the form of universality. But this universality had to take away from human nature all productive and engendering power." I admit that the Roman world had lost spiritual productivity and the capability of creative formations in state, religion, art, and science. But of what relevance is this loss when the issue is the physical conception of Jesus? At that time, pagan humanity lacked the power of producing a physical individual freely and purely out of itself, without the mediation of human intercourse. But humanity lacks this power not just because of the age and its specific circumstances, rather—it is ridiculous to have to say this—humanity never has it under any circumstances.

In the final analysis, this entire discussion is nothing but a trite and childish play with the proper and full meaning of the words [procreation] and productivity. To say that spiritually sterile paganism could not have produced out of itself in a literally physical way an individual makes as much sense as to say that when a book or a piece of research is called unfruitful, the logical question follows, "Thus, no seed will grow on it?"

Bauer also makes a judgement on Judaism. In spite of the fact that Judaism through its intuition of the divine nature as the truth of the human nature in the person of the Messiah had raised itself beyond the level of paganism and beyond the pain of the impotence of human nature in its abstract universality to bring itself to the real appearance of this idea, it was incapable of producing the God-man without the intervention of human intercourse. We will take Bauer

108

at his word on this without looking more closely at the proofs which he advances.

Bauer moves on to his conclusion in the following way: "Neither the sexual activity of individuals, nor human nature in its pure abstraction (the feeling of alienation from God in late antiquity), are in a position to produce the personality in which human nature exists in its pure universality, i.e., in its unity with its absolute essence. Moreover, the development of that personality in the religion of the Old Testament, since it is the religion of development, can never produce the presence of existence through itself. Therefore, human nature cannot effect unity with its absolute essence either for itself or in its pure movement to its absolute essence. Thus, the concept whose necessity for self-consciousness lies in that movement (the concept of the unity of the divine and human nature), could posit the real, existing expression of this necessity only through itself. The act in which it posits its appearance thus belongs to it originally and is itself an originating deed, a creation. Human nature in its separation from and in its relation to its truth could not positively contribute to this creation. All it could contribute was its receptivity.

109 And, indeed, in the woman, [or], more precisely, in the Virgin, this receptivity is present immediately, and the activity of the male is an activity that always has as its result the limitation of the outcome. Therefore, the human in whom the unity of the divine and human nature appeared had the Virgin for a mother and for his father the spirit who was the absolute necessity of the unity of divine and human nature. The God-man's existence is the result of the conjunction of receptivity and creative necessity."

No doubt Professor Bauer will not take offense at what I am going to say, because from his higher standpoint he understands that I cannot help but think as I do at my lower level. So I confess that, as often as I have read his treatment of Jesus' birth, still, with every new reading I think I am in the Faustian witches' kitchen and hearing:

An entire chorus
Of one hundred thousand fools speaking.

To contradict such arguments as these is not possible:
Because a total contradiction
Remains as mysterious for the wise as for the silly.

One can catch only the approximate meaning, and so one can only wonder how adventures of this kind can arise in a human brain.

At any rate, for Bauer, inasmuch as only something limited and incomplete is always produced by the sexual activities of individuals, the inception of the perfect and absolute personality of Christ must be grasped as an immediate act of universal human nature, without the help of human intercourse. And, since human nature as universal (and, to be sure, at the time of Jesus in the two forms of paganism and Judaism) is not productive for itself, the divine activity must enter into its receptivity in order to engender the God-man as its product. But what makes human nature in its universality incapable of physically engendering an individual out of itself is not its separation from the divine [such] that it would receive this capability by the intervention of God. The reason for this impotence is the exclusion of individuals without whose mediation human nature, whether separated from the divine or united with it, will never produce an individual.

Another reason why this production is not supposed to have taken place totally without human nature is given in the New Testament narrative itself in which a natural mother has a part in the conception of Jesus. Bauer explains that the receptivity given in humanity is directly present as a virgin. But one must ask: Why is not self-activity directly present as man? Then, through the union of both man and woman the required product would come into existence. Bauer has an answer. First, because the procreative activity of the man "always has as its result the limitation of the product." What is this? Does not the contribution that the woman makes toward producing a new living being have the same result? If a being begotten from a male seed can only be a limited, incomplete being, how can a being developed and born in the body of a woman be an absolute, perfect being?

Accepting Bauer's definition of the problem, which presupposes

110

the sinlessness of Jesus, as well as excluding the explanations he rejects as untenable, one is faced with a dilemma. If in order to have Christ originate as sinless it is found necessary to exclude the activity of the male in his conception, then for the same reason the activity of the female must be excluded also. Or, vice versa, if the activity of the female is not a hindrance, then neither is that of the male. But there is a second part to Bauer's answer. He thinks that a male's realized self-activity is not equal to a female's immediately posited receptivity in its potential to contribute to the conception of Christ because "human nature can contribute not positively, but only through its receptivity" to the production of the God-man.

111     Now, my head begins [to spin] again, and I start to imagine the witches' kitchen. All right, I do understand that, in relation to religion and to the ideal in general, humanity taken by itself does not relate productively, but rather receptively, to the divine spirit. However, the receptivity and productivity in question here are spiritual. Now, if the same logic is extended and one says that only the receptivity—the woman—and not equally human productivity—the man—contributed to the conception of the greatest religious personality, Jesus, then it would follow that humanity behaves merely receptively in the physical realm, too. But the only legitimate conclusion to be drawn from human spiritual receptivity is that it was not the activity of the parents as individuals who themselves endowed the son with this fullness of spirit, but rather the creative activity of the idea of humanity in its unification with the divinity. To claim that this activity had to have posited itself immediately in the place of the paternal contribution in the conception, as if to penetrate the mother with its power in the place of the sexual contribution of the father, is a palpable misunderstanding. Suppose it is true that human nature can produce by the mediation of individuals only that which is limited. Nevertheless, it would be the most violent alternative one could take if, in order to face the danger of recognizing limitation in the human appearance of Christ, one chose to break through the limits of physical impossibility.

Now you see the way I ought to have reasoned in order to understand the biblical history in its rationality and historical truth.

I confess that on this road of thought there is nothing so fantastic that it could not be made conceivable, or, indeed, could not be deduced. The school that acknowledges deductions of this type should not complain about the reproach of scholasticism.

Let me give an example of this type of deduction. To all poetry up to now adheres the limitation of its origin through single poets, who belong, moreover, to particular nations, times, and stages of culture. The idea of poetry, however, demands an absolute reali-                112
zation, which is to be attained only when it [gives] itself reality without the mediation of an individual who writes poetry. As individuals, humans cannot relate productively to the creation of this highest poetry; the human world can offer only pure receptivity. Now, since the receptivity for a poem entering upon actuality is immediately present as paper, it must happen once that the absolute poem must be written by poetry as such on the receptive paper without the intervention of a human hand.

An epilogue such as the one Professor Bauer gives to his deduction of the supernational conception of Christ could be added to this deduction: "In this conjunction of receptivity and creative necessity, all physiological questions are eliminated. They no longer have a place, not because they should be silenced in the face of a dark and inconceivable mystery, but on the contrary, because their finitude has also become manifest in the becoming-manifest(!) of the mystery."

I am passing over all of Professor Bauer's criticisms of my work that are not characteristic of his standpoint. In the course of these polemical writings I have already addressed or will address many of these criticisms. Now, I will turn to what Bauer says about miracles. "If understanding demands that one provide it with a way of contemplating a miracle, this demand is to be totally rejected. Since the process of miracle is immediate, it is purely inexplicable and not to be reflectively construed. Least of all is a basis for explanation to be retrieved from the analogy of nature."[64] This seems to end the matter quickly. We seem to be turned back from philosophy from which we sought an explanation to simple belief. Bauer does not intend

---

[64]Bauer, *JWK* (May 1836), no. 86, pp. 686f.

this. He assures us, "This does not mean that one must give up thinking about this subject and with thought the subject itself. For (1) insight that the miracle [cannot] be construed from the representation is to be obtained only through the concept, and (2) the inexplicability of the miracle means only that it is to be explained from nothing but its own personal principle."

According to Professor Bauer, the concept of miracle from which the insight into its lack of representability should flow is: miracle "is different from the common course of nature, not only relatively, but absolutely"; (as already mentioned) "the process of miracle is immediate," and, therefore, "not to be reflectively construed"; in miracle there are to be identified no "natural stages" which it runs through by chance at top speed.

But this alleged concept of miracle is nonsense. (If I said it was a "contradiction," Professor Bauer would no doubt remind me that if "only that which is without contradiction were true and actual, this honor would be due only to the dead and simple. In all life, the higher its stage, the deeper the contradiction it bears within it, but the concept contains the deepest contradiction of all."[65]) An "immediate process" is no less an oxymoron than immediate mediation. I can think of a mediation raising itself to immediacy, but the stages to be traversed in it, even if lowered to sublated moments, can still be identified. In Bauer's concept of miracle, no stages are to be traversed, and yet a process is supposed to be present. Maybe we are arguing about a word. Maybe the author uses the expression "process" only in a completely indefinite sense, and then drops it as soon as he remembers that it is incompatible with the adjective "immediate." If we continue to hold onto this immediacy, and still add to it the other part of Bauer's proposition—that miracles are distinct from the common course of nature not just relatively, but absolutely—the nonsense only stands out all the more.

The (presupposed) miracle occurs within nature, but certainly not in such a way that it brings along with it its own characteristic matter and merely [spreads] this on the ground of nature. Miracle takes its material from the content of nature, and itself imparts

[65] Ibid., p. 684.

merely its own form, or new relationships, and so on. Thus, for miracle to be absolutely different from the course of nature is inconceivable. The natural object may be treated differently by the miracle worker than by a merely natural influence, but it will in both cases be treated as an object of nature. An influence that took no account at all of the natural object's quality as natural could not touch it or cause anything to happen to it. It follows from this that in miraculous activity two sides can be distinguished: one that is conditioned by the peculiarity of this action, and another that is conditioned by the peculiarity of the object to which it is directed. But that the property of this object is natural necessarily entails that any change produced in it must be mediate. According to its concept, nature is existence that is dispersed into individuation, in which each moment, although connected to the others, also has an existence on its own.

For example, the human body is this manifold of vessels, muscles, nerves and bones, members and organs. More precisely, the eye is not just this single unity which we name, but it is just as much a reality made up of parts such as membranes and fluids which are external to one another. Moreover, these parts exist in connection with other parts of the body such as the brain, and the like. Thus, whoever wants to have an effect on the eye, say, to heal blindness, does not face a single unity that he can change immediately with one act. Rather he must treat the eye as it functions, that is, as this plurality of moments which his action has to traverse, and thus his action has to assume the character of mediation.

Even the miracle worker cannot escape this necessity of mediation which is inherent in the object. Otherwise, one would have to say that the object was changed before the miracle worker affected it so that it no longer behaved naturally. This is new nonsense! Obviously, this change is also an effect and, as an effect [on] a natural object, it can take place only in the mode of mediation.        115

Consequently, the supernaturalist interpreters are not as totally wrong in their treatment of miracles as Bauer would say they are. Especially in more recent times, they have tried to stress the side of necessary mediation in the biblical miracles and to explain them as processes. For this purpose they have used particularly the category of an accelerated process of nature. According to them, the conjunction of the supernatural, and thus superpowerful, force with an object of nature actually can only result in the more fluid interaction of the various aspects of the natural object. Thus, the process, which the effect must traverse in stages, moves with less contradiction and more speed than it would ordinarily. Many of the biblical miracles, especially those of healing, can be understood in this way. Because this interpretation cannot account for other miracles, such as the multiplication of the loaves and the changing of water into wine, Bauer was precipitous in abandoning it entirely.

To console us further about the incomprehensibility of miracles, Professor Bauer gives the second argument that this incomprehensibility only means: "Miracle is to be explained out of nothing but its personal principle." We are told that "in individual products of nature the universal law of nature works in the form of a single, limited law, whereas miracle is the activity of the universal and absolute law working through the self-consciousness that has become one with it. As this action, it is a creation freely willed by spirit. It is true that the laws of nature are the eternal ideas and determinations of the will of God, but nature reveals the divine ideas immanent to it only in the finite form of divided being. If nature's inner movement proves single laws to be finite and sublates them, still natural law as such is not sublated but confirmed. For it is spirit which [proves] itself to be the absolute law of nature through this movement. Even in the miracle, then, this law of nature is neither violated nor interrupted, but it is revealed in its totality and its unity with the individual will." The only personal principle that can explain miracle is therefore the self-consciousness of Christ, which became one with the absolute divine law. As Professor Bauer himself knows, all that directly follows from this unity between Christ's self-consciousness and the absolute divine law is that in his relation to nature the God-man would accept the divine will as his own. But God wills the law of nature, and thus, the God-man would abstain from any interference with this law that would lie outside the boundaries of ordered human action on it.

So Bauer denigrates as imperfect the way the divine idea is realized in the common course of nature. The natural law works in the regular course of nature only in the form of individual limited laws (the law of gravity, of electricity, of chemical processes, of organic life, and so on). In contrast to this, the God-man brings to reality the universal and absolute law of nature, the spirit as power over this law. This presentation lacks the one element that would make it convincing. Bauer does not prove that ordinary human actions on nature are not, at least to some extent, the true activation of the power of spirit over it, and thus he does not prove that the God-man must activate this power, or that he has to activate it in at least a higher manner than others. Until such a proof is forthcoming, I stand by my proposition—the victory that humanity wins by culture over nature within itself and by inventions or machines over nature outside of itself is of more value than any victory over nature won by a mere word of a *Thaumaturgen*.

Professor Bauer's treatment of the resurrection of Jesus is also characteristic of his standpoint. Paradoxically, he does not find it [difficult] to imagine Jesus' revivification, but rather to imagine his actual death. Obviously, he does not have his problem with Jesus' death because a revivification would have to follow it, but because of the concept of the person of Jesus.[66] This is his difficulty: "If Christ is the perfect personality, then there is nothing that could be called an abstract other over against him, nothing that he had not subordinated to spirit and fully penetrated with spirit. For Christ, the distinction, which still applies to us in the present, between the spiritual body and the body not yet subordinated to spirit was continually sublated. For Christ, the conflict with other-being, of externality against the penetrating power of spirit, was swallowed up, uninterrupted, in the victory of spirit. In our own lives death is the principal proof that this victory of spirit over the abstraction of externality has indeed begun, but is not yet complete. The finite relation of spirit to that which is not yet absolutely united to it is sublated in death and is given over to the fate of its finitude, to destruction. But, since this relation of spirit to body was complete

117

---

[66]Ibid., pp. 699ff.

in the person of Jesus, it seems that his personality could not be absolutely lost by death."

Following this argumentation in another direction, one comes upon Professor Bauer flirting with the danger of assuming a merely apparent death of Jesus. He writes: "Since Jesus entered into suffering with absolute willingness, this suffering at its peak was not distinct from his infinite activity. But if his most extreme suffering is immediately united with the counterthrust of his innermost activity, then, in the midst of death, his relation to his body seems to remain uninterrupted." Apparently, Bauer himself feels that his deductions from the concept of the person of Christ have taken him too far. These prove not just the necessity of the resurrection of Jesus, but also the impossibility of his death. What follows from Bauer's representation of Jesus as the one in whom spirit has completely empowered corporeality and has thus removed it from the influence of any external force? Not that the [bond] between Jesus' body and soul, which is severed in death, must be joined again, but rather that the bond could never be completely dissolved.

To avoid this conclusion, Professor Bauer states: "The process of absolute reaction in the suffering of Christ should not be understood to be immediate; otherwise, it is not a process. (Incidentally, we see here that my opponent grants the point I just used against him, i.e., that a process is inconceivable as immediate.) If one finds this process to be immediate, one flirts with the danger of Docetism. The death of Jesus was a real death, the separation of body and soul. But since the perfected personality had united its corporeality to itself in complete agreement, its relation to corporeality could well be interrupted, but it could not be abstractly lost. On the contrary, spirit fulfilled and restored the unity of his body and soul. Christ through the immanent process of his personality was not only reawakened, but resurrected."

What does it mean not to have to think of the reaction of the divine spiritual activity against suffering in Christ as immediate? It can only mean, according to what we have read, that the counterthrust of activity against suffering did not always step in instantly at each time. It does not mean that this activity had to allow suffering

118

to become actual. All that can be concluded from this is that Jesus did not pull back the part of him capable of suffering from suffering itself. He allowed suffering into himself and overcame it. But if he was to be in absolute control of his body, he could not lose complete control of it—in my terms—that is, he could not die. Furthermore, this view, which places the goal of the power of the spirit over the body in immortality because it presupposes a gradual physical glorification of the body in Christ, runs into the kind of fanaticism shown by Olshausen, which I have discussed in other places.[67]

Professor Bauer objects to my assertion, which I made in the dogmatic conclusion of *The Life of Jesus*, that it is in no way the mode of the idea to lavish all its fullness on a single exemplar and to be stingy toward all the rest.[68] He responds: "Neither the doctrine of the Church [nor] speculation assert this. One single human is not separated out as the actuality of the idea, and the total humanity excluded from it. On the contrary, humanity is enclosed and encompassed in this actuality of the idea: thus the exclusivity of this personality is sublated, and the incarnation of God becomes eternal" (apparently by means of the Holy Spirit, which disperses what is given in Christ across humanity).

But this entire bit of information, as often as it also has made itself visible elsewhere as an argument against critique,[69] is still only an empty polemic about words, which is rooted in an almost deliberate misunderstanding. Naturally, I do not deny that church doctrine, as well as the speculation that conforms to it, grants a share in the divine humanity to the rest of humanity outside of Christ. I deny only that it finds this divine humanity to be realized perfectly in Christ and merely imperfectly in all other humans. To me an outpouring of the total fullness of the idea into one individual, and a stinginess toward the rest, is incompatible with the way the idea is otherwise realized. Given every difference in the portion of the

119

---

[67][See above, p. 7]
[68][See Strauss, *Das Leben Jesu*, 2:734.]
[69]For example, in the review of my *Life of Jesus* by Ullmann in *Theologische Studien und Kritiken* 3 (1836): 811f.

idea in individuals, it still realizes itself in such a manner that each individual in turn needs to be complemented through others.[70]

Finally, the following remarks can still shed some light on the position taken on the general view of the gospel history by this reviewer of my *Life of Jesus* for the *Jahrbücher für wissenschaftliche Kritik*. He said that "the book would still be valuable, if Professor Strauss had shown nothing more than that the mythical view, even if applied to only one gospel passage, will spin around and gobble up the entire narrative. The same canon that critique demands for the beginning of the life of Jesus applies to the end and to the middle."[71] [Here] we have the same dilemma as that posed in the *Evangelische Kirchenzeitung*: either retain everything as historical, or all of it collapses as unhistorical! We also have materially the same decision inside of the dilemma, that is, a decision for the side: retain everything as history.

The variation between the positions of Bauer and that of the *Evangelische Kirchenzeitung* is merely formal. He entertains critique and doubt in general for a while, in order to turn them around secretly to affirm the gospel history. We have now seen well enough how this reversal is accomplished—with words and more words, words which, just when concepts fail, appear at the right time, words which promise to bring themselves, with a mighty propulsion, above the grave, and to take us along with our eyes closed. But, in reality, these words, no matter how high they leap, always remain on this side of the grave.

## 2. The Center of the Hegelian School

This position, following our initial definition, includes those Hegelian theologians who would modify the right-wing assertion that the entire gospel history is given with the idea of the unity of

---

[70]See the explanation that I inserted into the second edition of my *Life of Jesus* about this. [D. F. Strauss, *Das Leben Jesu, kritisch bearbeitet*, 2 vols. (Tübingen: Osiander, 1837), 2:739. In the first edition Strauss stated: "This is indeed not the mode in which Idea realizes itself; it is not wont to lavish all its fullness on one exemplar and be stingy towards all the rest. It rather loves to distribute its riches among a multiplicity of exemplars which reciprocally complete each other." In the second edition he inserted after the first sentence the phrase: "to express itself perfectly in one individual, and imperfectly in all the rest."]

[71]See Bauer, *JWK* (December 1836), no. 111, p. 889.

divine and human nature. These theologians assert that at least one part of this history, its principal and focal point, is guaranteed as historical by the idea. Because of the dominance of its conservative wing, only a few members of the Hegelian school belong to the center. Among those who have spoken out publically and scientifically about gospel history, I can only really name Rosenkranz.

Rosenkranz is a Hegelian who is worthy of a great deal of attention and who brings honor to the school. The clarity and liveliness of his spirit fight against the inclination to formalistic ossification, which, because of the academic training in Hegelian philosophizing, is prevalent in this school. His versatility checks the narrowness and tastelessness that we have found in much contemporary thought, and which touched the Hegelian philosophy in only one specific area. Finally, with true liberality, which he [inherited] in the school of Schleiermacher, and which he made better use of than most of the other Hegelian theologians, he repeatedly has come to the defense of embattled publications. He seeks to protect works attacked by an irrational zeal, which ignores the true and the good in favor of the uncouth lie. The rest of the public, sight unseen, or fearfully and pharisaically, condemns these books because of the cry of a few defenders of Zion.[72] Thus, we can expect that Rosenkranz, even on the question of gospel history, will not try to dispatch us with hollow formulas, or keep us within the constraints of an ignorant standpoint, or lead us anxiously and hypocritically around the difficult passages.

121

"All the contradictions," Rosenkranz remarks, "that the external history of Christ hands to us can be readily acknowledged. Indeed, one must acknowledge them or commit intellectual suicide.[73] Philosophy cannot allow itself the desire to deduce the miraculous events in the life of Christ. To try that, however honorably and religiously, would be to do much more harm than good to religion itself. But philosophy can say how it finds reason, the *a priori*, expressed in he *a posteriori*, historical existence. So it must find it to be fully rational

---

[72][Press censorship under the Carlsbad decrees was especially strict after the Paris Revolution of 1830. Not only overt political works were censored, but theologically unorthodox works were also suppressed.]

[73]Rosenkranz, *Kritik*, p. xviii.

when, according to tradition, Christ is said to have had no human
father and to have ascended to heaven. Such facts contradict everything that philosophy knows; they do not fit its concepts, and, from
love of the truth, philosophy must be proud enough not to rush in
with accommodations though it is at liberty to point out how the
fact that the unity of the divine with the human is not merely
momentary and transient but everlasting cannot be expressed more
clearly than by the fact of the ascension."[74]

122        [Presumably,] Rosenkranz does not mean to say here that philosophy can construe this fact merely *a priori*. Rather, if the fact is
presented to philosophy, as in the life of Jesus, it is able not only
to grasp its meaning reflectively, but also to recognize it in its historical truth. That he intends to surrender the historical character
of such narratives is made clear in his comment on Schleiermacher's
famous assertion that nothing definite can be conceived from the
phrases of the Creed—"to be conceived by the Holy Spirit" and "to
descend into hell." Rosenkranz says, "If Schleiermacher wanted to
ask, 'What, then, do you think about these phrases, which are empty
for me?' I would immediately answer that what I think about the
reception of Christ by the Holy Spirit is that the only principle of
the life of Christ was the divine spirit which defined his will and
through his will his nature. And when I consider the meaning of
the descent into hell, I think that all evil even before the appearance
of Christ is real only through opposition because in itself it is nothing.
It only has significance through the good that it attempts to negate.
At the same time, good is the only essence to which evil, in order
to flee from its hell, can raise itself. But Christ, as the one who only
wills the good, is the one who also descends into evil to free freedom
by means of the pain of opposition from the chains of the evil will
and to return that will to its true essence.

On the other hand, if Schleiermacher wanted to say, 'Look,
here you have given me a completely rationalistic interpretation of
the dogma, for you seem to believe in neither a sensible appearance
(and agency) of the Holy Spirit, nor a sensibly existing hell. You

---

[74]Karl Rosenkranz, "Eine Parallele zur Religionsphilosphie," *Zeitschrift für speculative
Theologie*, vol. 2, bk. 1, p. 29.

understand the conception as well as the descent into hell to mean
that the will of Christ was absolute and holy from the beginning.
Thus these phrases mean that only Christ is in a position to be free
as if from sin as from the pain that sin engenders as negation of
freedom, and that even before the founding of Christianity [as] a
phenomenon, this relation between good and evil was there.'—to
this we would answer, 'Be that as it may, we were lucky to find
without sophistry or forcing a meaning something very definite expressed in these representations as they are given to us.' So if
Schleiermacher wants to call rationalistic such a procedure of clearly
thinking the universal and eternal content of these representations,
which were initally historically based, we do not object. We are of
the firm opinion that true Christianity is rational and that reason is
Christian."[75]

Here Rosenkranz uses what he thinks is the conceptual content
of these credal phrases to avoid the issue of whether the historical
reality of those parts of the life of Jesus to which these phrases refer
has become unthinkable or at least doubtful for him.

The following explanation leaves no doubt after all about his
real intention. "The understanding, which remains caught in the
illusion of an external relation between cause and effect, identifies
the cause for the holiness of Christ to be the spirit of God, as if the
spirit naturally and sensibly (something clearly supermystical and
inconceivable) engendered Christ. Now it is clear that Christ as the
Son of God and as Savior of the world has no other father than the
divine spirit and that, from *this perspective*, he is engendered only by
the spirit and not by a human. But it is precisely because here only
the true spirit has meaning, that the other side, that of natural birth,
is of a subordinate significance."[76] In any case, an *a priori* deduction
of the supernatural conception of Jesus such as that Professor Bauer
gave is as nonsensical to Rosenkranz as it is to me.

At least, Rosenkranz does not believe he must affirm as historical
the miracles in the Gospels—at least not all of them. He says, "In
the history of [Christ,] one must distinguish those miracles that

123

124

---

[75]Rosenkranz, *Kritik*, pp. 111f.
[76]Rosenkranz, *Enzyklopädie*, p. 151.

happen to Christ from those that happen through him. These two kinds of miracles form two entirely separate domains. The passive miracles (such as the heavenly voices praising Christ and his ascension, among others) have more of a mythical character and are much rarer than the active miracles, which are principally healings of the sick, especially of those whose disease is spiritual confusion. Some of the miracles, such as the turning of water into wine, walking on the sea, the curse of the fig tree, catching the stater in the fish's mouth—apart from their excellent poetry and meaning—contradict all reason to such an extent that nothing is left to do with them other than to admit their inconceivability."[77]

Making all these concessions to critique, says Rosenkranz, "cannot damage the subject matter in itself, the actuality of the idea in its appearance (in Christ)." To be sure, "in and for itself all of history, in spite of the evil it contains, is always grasped as the process of the incarnation of God both before and after the appearance of Jesus. History cannot be arrested with Jesus as a single being of the past, because the compression of the eternally self-identical idea into that one life, which already took place, would be a make-believe knowing that would put external limits on the infinite life of God." And yet it remains certain "that this single shape whose memory history has offered us so that we can still present to ourselves a picture of its immediate life—that it alone and no other human was adequate to the concept and that it fulfilled the reality of the idea as an individual appearance. From this perspective, Jesus alone is the only begotten Son of God who in the appearance of Christ posits himself as a discrete existence in an absolute manner. In this genuine singleness the idea establishes the proof of its actuality, and divine nature [has] therefore proven itself in reality to be the truth of human nature."

From this point on Rosenkranz like Bauer tries to deduce[78] the miraculous deeds of Christ (inasmuch as he finds only one kind of the gospel miracle accounts to be historically questionable). What I have just cited must have been a criticism of me because Rosenkranz immediately remarks, "I see the basic mistake of Strauss's conception

---

[77]Ibid., p. 161.
[78]Ibid., pp. 160f.

to be that he wishes to assert the subjectivity of substance only in the infinite variety of subjects, in the human species. Christ is no collective unity of predicates which the spirit of humanity imparted to him; he is the concrete unity of these."[79]

The proof of this assertion is only intimated and not thoroughly developed in these propositions: "The essence of the idea includes within itself precisely the *absoluteness* of the appearance as individual, as *this* single human. The thought of seeing Christ in humanity achieves its full truth only at first through the mediation of the absolute incarnation of God, and it is by no means sublated by this mediation." We reject the latter proposition as we did before. We deny that because of the imperfection of each single human a realization of the divine in humanity in general would not be a true incarnation. The former statement is a paralogism, which rests on the confusion of *the* single and *a* single. It is in the essence of the idea that it appears in *the* singles and that it makes human individuals into the bearers of its absolute content, because, as Hegel says, the ultimate pinnacle of spirit is precisely individuality, subjectivity.

But that any *one single* individual must be exclusively the full realization of the idea is not found in the essence of the idea. At the very least, Rosenkranz's argument here is no better than the [one]    126 in his *Encyclopedia of Theological Science* to the effect that Christ remains unique "because history, as nature, repeats itself in contingent occurrences but not in necessary ones, that is, history acts superfluously. Thus, to engender still another Christ as an individual phenomenon would be just as superfluous as to engender a new Adam, new natural humans."[80]

This much is probably given in the essence of the idea: that human individuals in general, just like individuals in all the natural and spiritual realms, are not the only ones to relate themselves differently to the idea as more or less complete expressions of it; but also that, more definitely, what is characteristic of history is that a series of individuals emerge as geniuses who shape and determine epochs for other humans; and finally that in religion, as the mediation

---

[79]Rosenkranz, *Kritik*, p. xvii, n. 31.
[80]Rosenkranz, *Enzyklopädie*, p. 39.

of the human with the divine, an individual can be thought of who has attained the goal of this mediation, the inclusion of both the divine and the human in self-consciousness—but only the conceivability, not the necessity, of such an individual can be deduced. Moreover, that Jesus was in fact just this individual, and that only he and no one else before or after him has attained this *non plus ultra* of religious development, cannot be established by philosophy but only by the discipline of history.

I separate from Rosenkranz, with the assertion that the truth of the gospel history is not to be liberated by philosophy, either as a whole or in part, but only by the investigation of the same by historical critique. Thus I would have passed over to

## 3. The Left Wing of the Hegelian School

if this school had not advanced to exclude me completely from its anks and to throw me into other intellectual camps—of course, only to catch me when, just like a ball, I was thrown back again.

# SELECTED BIBLIOGRAPHY

*The Christ of Faith and the Jesus of History.* Translated by Leander Keck. Philadelphia: Fortress Press, 1977.

*The Life of Jesus, Critically Examined.* Edited and with an introduction by Peter C. Hodgson. Translated from the fourth German edition by George Eliot. Philadelphia: Fortress Press, 1972.

On Strauss

Cromwell, Richard S. *David Friedrich Strauss and His Place in Modern Thought.* Fair Lawn, N.J.: R. E. Burdick, 1974.

Harris, Horton. *David Friedrich Strauss and His Theology.* Cambridge: Cambridge University Press, 1973.

Massey, Marilyn Chapin. *Christ Unmasked: The Meaning of "The Life of Jesus" in German Politics.* Chapel Hill, N.C.: University of North Carolina Press, 1983.

With Significant Treatments of Strauss

Barth, Karl. *From Rousseau to Ritschl.* London: S. M. C. Press, 1959.

Nietzsche, Friedrich Wilhelm. *On the Advantage and Disadvantage of History for Life.* Translated and with an introduction by Peter Preuss. Indianapolis: Hackett Publishing Company, 1980.

Schweitzer, Albert. *The Quest of the Historical Jesus.* Translated by W. Montgomery. New York: MacMillan, 1964.

## *Works in German*

By Strauss

*Die christliche Glaubenslehre in ihrer geschichtlichen Entwicklung und im Kampfe mit der modernen Wissenschaft.* 2 vols. Tübingen: Osiander,

1840-41. Reprint ed., Frankfurt: Minerva Gmbh, Wissenschaft-licher Verlag und Buchhandlung, 1982.

*Der Christus des Glaubens und der Jesus der Geschichte.* Berlin: Franz Duncker, 1865.

*Gesammelte Schriften von David Friedrich Strauss. Nach der Verfassers letzwilligen Bestimmungen zusammengestellt.* 12 vols. Edited by Eduard Zeller. Bonn: Fromann, 1876-78.

*Das Leben Jesu, kritisch bearbeitet.* 2 vols. Tübingen: Osiander, 1835-36. 2d rev. ed. 2 vols. Tübingen: Osiander, 1837. 3rd rev. ed. 2 vols. Tübingen: Osiander, 1838. 4th rev. ed. 2 vols. Tübingen: Osiander, 1839-40.

*Streitschriften zur Verteidigung meiner Schrift über das Leben Jesus und zur Charakteristik der gegenwärtigen Theologie.* 3 parts. Tübingen: Osiander, 1837. Reprint ed. 3 vols. in 1. New York: G. Olms, 1980.

Strauss's Major Sources for *In Defense*

Bauer, Bruno. "Rezension Strauss, Das Leben Jesu." *Jahrbücher für wissenschaftliche Kritik*, 2(1835): 879-94, 879-912; 1(1836): 681-94, 697-704.

————. "Rezension von Schriften über Strauss' Leben Jesu." *Jahrbücher für wissenschaftliche Kritik*, 1(1837): 321-43.

Baur, Ferdinand Christian. *Die christliche Gnosis: oder, Die christliche Religions-Philosophie in ihrer geschichtlichen Entwicklung.* Tübingen: Osiander, 1835.

Gabler, G. A. *De Verae philosophiae erga religionem christianam pietate.* Berlin: Duncker and Humbolt, 1836.

Göschel, Carl. *Aphorismen über Nichtwissen und absolutes Wissen im Verhältnis zur christlichen Glaubenserkenntnis.* Berlin: Franklin, 1829.

Hegel, G. W. F. *Grundlinien der Philosophie des Rechts.* Berlin: Nicolai, 1821.

————. *System der Wissenschaft: Erster Teil, die Phänomenologie des Geistes.* Bamberg and Würzburg: J. A. Goebhardt, 1807.

————. *Vorlesungen über die Geschichte der Philosophie,* ed. D. Karl Ludwig Michelet. 3 vols. Berlin: Duncker and Humbolt, 1833-36.

————. *Vorlesungen über die Philosophie der Religion.* 3 vols. in 2. Vols. 11 and 12 of *Werke: Vollständige Ausgabe durch einen Verein von Freunden des Verewigten.* 18 vols. Berlin: Duncker and Humbolt, 1832-45.

Rosenkranz, Karl. *Enzyklopädie der theologischen Wissenschaft.* Halle: C. A. Schwetschke, 1831.

————. *Kritik der Schleiermacherschen Glaubenslehre.* Königsberg: Gebrüder Bornträger, 1836.

Schelling, Friedrich. *Vorlesungen über die Methode des academischen Studiums.* Stuttgart and Tübingen: J. G. Cotta, 1830.

Schleiermacher, Friedrich. *Das Leben Jesu.* Edited by K. A. Rütenik. Division 1, vol. 6. in *Sämmtliche Werke.* 3 divisions. 31 vols. Berlin: Reimer, 1835-64.

Ullmann, Karl. "Rezension. D. F. Strauss, Leben Jesu." *Theologische Studien und Kritiken* 9(1836): 770-816.

## Recent Books on Strauss and the Hegelian School

Cornehl, Peter. *Die Zukunft der Versöhnung: Eschatologie und Emanzipation in der Aufklärung, bei Hegel und in der Hegelschen Schule.* Göttingen: Vandenhoeck and Ruprecht, 1971.

Gebhardt, Jürgen. *Politik und Eschatologie: Studien zur Geschichte der Hegelschen Schule in den Jahren 1830-1840.* Münchener Studien zur Politik. Vol. 1. Munich: C. H. Beck, 1963.

Graf, F. W. *Kritik und Pseudo-Spekulation, David Friedrich Strauss als Dogmatiker im Kontext der positionellen Theologie Seiner Zeit.* Munich: Kaiser, Chr. Verlag, 1981.

Jaeschke, Walter. "Urmenschheit und Monarchie: Eine politische Christologie der Hegelschen Rechten." *Hegel-Studien.* Edited by Friedhelm Nicolin and Otto Pöggeler. Vol. 14. Bonn: Bouvier Verlag Herbert Grundmann, 1979.

Lange, Dietz. *Historischer Jesu oder mythischer Christus: Untersuchungen zu dem Gegensatz zwischen Friedrich Schleiermacher und David Friedrich Strauss.* Gütersloh: Gütersloher Verlagshaus G. Mohr, 1975.

Müller, Gotthold. *Identität und Immanenz: Zur Genese der Theologie von David Friedrich Strauss.* Zurich: EVZ-Verlag, 1968.

Sandberger, Jorg F. *David Friedrich Strauss als theologischer Hegelianer.* Göttingen: Vandenhoeck and Ruprecht, 1972.

Theunissen, Michael. *Hegels Lehre vom absoluten Geist als theologisch-politischer Trakat.* Berlin: Walter de Gruyter, 1970.

# INDEX

Absolute religion, xxix, xxxiv, 9, 21
Absolute spirit, xxii–xxiv, xxix–xxx,
  24, 28
Absolute truth, xxiv, xxix, 11, 26
Alienation, 22, 24, 25, 29, 31, 34, 50
Ascension, xxxii, 35, 62
Bauer, Bruno, xxii–xxxv, 43–60, 63, 64
Baur, Ferdinand Christian, xxxvii n.4
Believing certainty, 23, 27, 29
Believing consciousness, xxx, 11–13,
  21, 24–26, 30, 32, 35
Center Hegelians. *See* Hegelian school
Christ of faith, xi, xiv, xix, xxx, 25,
  32
Comic, xxxii
Concept (*Begriff*), xxix, xxxi, 3–5, 29,
  31–33, 37–39, 47, 54, 63; and gospel
  history, 3–5
Conception of Jesus, 34, 46, 48, 49
Contingency, xxxv, 47, 48, 65
Critique, the nature of, xxxv, xxxvi, 9–
  11, 20, 37, 39, 43–45, 48; as Hege-
  lian, xxvii, xxxiii–xxxiv; of religion,
  xxxiv, xxxvi. *See also* Historical
  critique
Dogma, xx, 5, 11–13, 31, 34, 35, 38
Death of God, 28
Death of Jesus, xxx–xxxii, 25, 26, 28–
  30, 35, 58
Feuerbach, Ludwig, x, xxvi
Fichte, Johann Gottlieb, xxii, 8, 9, 12
Gabler, Georg Andreas, xii, xxxiii, 41,
  43
God as love, 27, 32
God-man, xx, xxvii, xxx–xxxiii, 19, 23,
  28–29, 35, 51–52, 56–57
Göschel, Carl Friedrich, xii, xxiii–
  xxxiv, xxxvii n.8, 4, 38–43

Gospels, historical validity of, xii, xiv–
  xvi, xix, xxvi, xxxii, xxxv, 3, 5, 12,
  14, 21, 33–34, 37; and Fourth Gospel, 6, 19
Greco-Roman world, xxx
Hegel, Georg Wilhelm Friedrich, ix;
  critique of Kant, xxii; *Encyclopedia*, 9–
  10; *Logic*, 10; *Phenomenology of Spirit*,
  xxiii, xxvi, xxxviii n.27, 3, 10–11, 13
Hegelian philosophy, and Prussian politics, xi–xiii
Hegelian school, 19; center, xiii–xvi,
  xxvi, xxxiii, xxxv, 38; left-wing, x,
  xiii, xxvii, xxxiii–xxxv, 38; right-
  wing, xii–xiii, xvi, xxvi, xxxii, xxxiv–
  xxxv, 38, 43, 47
Hegelian terminology. *See* Absolute religion; Absolute spirit; Absolute
  truth; Alienation; Believing certainty;
  Believing consciousness; Concept (*Begriff*); Immediacy; Incarnation; Individuality; Necessity; Particularity;
  Philosophy and religion; Reason (*Vernunft*); Receptivity; Religion; Religious representation (*Vorstellung*); Self
  consciousness; Singularity; Subjectivity; Sublation (*Aufhebung*); Substance;
  Universality; World historical
  individual
Heine, Heinrich, ix, xii
Historical critique, xiii, xv, xix, xxvi,
  xxxii–xxxiii, xxxv, 14, 19, 20, 66;
  Hegel on, 8; presuppositions of,
  xxxiv, 44–46
Historical verification, xxxi, 32–35. *See
  also* Gospels, historical validity of
Hodgson, Peter C., xxxviii n.27
Humanity, xxi, 15, 30, 52
Human nature, 47–49, 51

Human species, xi, xxi, xxv, xxvii, xxxiii, xxxiv

Immediacy, xxvii, xxxi, 28, 37, 53–55, 58; and certainty, 21; and intuition, xxiii, 10–12

Incarnation, xiv, xxiv–xxv, xxvii–xxxii, xxxv, 12, 16–24, 30, 31, 36, 64–65; idea of, xxiv, xxv, xxvii–xxviii, 42–43, 59–60, 65

Individuality, 22, 30, 41, 65

Jesus, historical, xi, xiv, xxx, 25, 32; consciousness of, xxvii, xxx, 19; as accidental occasion for the Incarnation, xxx, 27; words of, 19, 26, 36; as teacher, 21, 26. See also Ascension; Conception of Jesus; Death of Jesus; Resurrection; Virgin birth

Judaism, 49, 51

Kant, Immanuel, xii, xxi–xxii, 9–10, 43; on the idea of humanity, xxi, xxv; on the Son of God, xxi; on kingdom of God, 27–28; The Critique of Pure Reason, xxi, xxvi. See also Subjectivism

Left-wing Hegelians. See Hegelian school

Lessing, Gotthold, xi

Life of Jesus, Critically Examined, impact of, x–xiii; summary of, xiii–xxv

Marheineke, Philip Conrad, xiv, 4, 5

Marx, Karl, ix, x, xii, xiii

Miracles, xiv, xvii, xxxii, 19, 26, 34, 35, 53–56, 61, 63; of healing, 56, 64

Mohammed, 17

Mohammedans, 21

Myth, x, xi, xvi, xvii, xix, xxi, 33, 64

Mythical interpretation, xviii–xix, 60

Naturalists, xvi

Necessity, xxxv, 47, 48, 65

Need, xx, 25–27, 37

Neoplatonists, 24, 25

Niebuhr, Barthold G., 8

Nodal point, 41

Olshausen, Hermann, 7, 59

Orthodox Christology, xx, xxxiii–xxxiv, 14, 19, 47, 59

Orthodoxy, xi, 4, 14, 19

Paganism, 49, 51

Pantheism, 14, 30

Particularity, 23, 29, 30

Paulus, H. E. G., xviii, 7

Philosophy and religion, xxiii, 12

Positivism, xxvi–xxvii, xxxiii–xxxiv, 43

Rationalists, xvi, xviii–xix, xxxii

Realism, xxxiv, 43

Reason (Vernunft), xxi–xxii

Receptivity, 50–53

Religion, xiv, xxiv, xxix, 15–18, 38

Religious genius, xxvii–xxviii, xxxv, 17, 19

Religious representation (Vorstellung), xiv–xvi, xix–xx, xxiv, xxix, xxxi, xxxv, 3–4, 21, 28–31, 35–36, 38–41, 48, 54, 63; and history, 3–5

Resurrection, xxxii, 6, 35, 57–58

Right-wing Hegelians. See Hegelian school

Roman world, 49

Rosenkrancz, Karl, xiii, xxxiii, xxxv, 6, 15, 61–66

Schelling, Friedrich, xxii, xxiii, xxvi, xxxiii, 8–13, 22, 37–38

Schleiermacher, Friedrich, xiii, 6, 11, 46, 61–63

Self consciousness, xxii, 21, 22, 24, 28–30, 34–35, 44, 45, 56, 66

Sense certainty, 11, 13, 23, 32, 33

Sinfulness of Christ, 47, 52

Singularity, 14, 15; of Christ, xxiv–xxv, xxx, 23, 28, 30–31, 37, 40, 42–43, 48, 59, 64–65

Socrates, xxix, 16, 21, 26, 27

Son of God, xx, xxxi, 32, 41, 63, 64

Spinoza, Baruch, xxiv

Subjectivism, xxii, xxvii, xxxiii–xxxiv, 9; and Kant, xxix, xxxiii, 8, 14–15; and Schleiermacher, 14

Subjectivity, xxiii, 22, 30, 65

Sublation (Aufhebung), 3, 13, 29, 36, 42

Substance, 22, 24, 34

Supernaturalists, xvi, xvii, xix, xxxii, 43, 55, 56

Theological critique, xxxiv

Theological phenomenology, 11

Tholuck, Friedrich August Gottreu, 6

Trinity, 26, 31, 32

Ullmann, Karl, 6

Understanding (Verstand), xxi–xxii, 22, 63

Universality, xxxi, 23, 29, 31, 50

Virgin birth, xvii–xviii, xxxii, 46–53

World historical individual, xxvii, 15